The

# DANCE

of the

# GIFTS

*How Ministry Leaders Can
Discern God's Will*

MARK R. BARNARD
KENNETH QUICK

ISBN: 9781654567507
Independently Published

"In *The Dance of the Gifts*, Mark Barnard and Ken Quick have provided a helpful way of seeing how the diversity of gifts in the body of Christ should and can enhance our unity as brothers and sisters in Christ. As the grace of the gospel enables us to remain humble, we are then able to hear and learn from one another as we speak from the perspective of our own gifting. This book is accessible, practical and biblical. After reading this book, it will change how you view other Christians and the gifts they each have been given for the common good."

**Dr. Tim S Lane**
President, Institute for Pastoral Care
Author of *Unstuck: A Nine-Step Journey to Change That Lasts* and *Living Without Worry: How to Replace Anxiety with Peace*

"Pastors and church leaders sometimes fail to consider how the Lord speaks through the giftedness of the members of the body. *The Dance of the Gifts* offers valuable insights into the importance and use of spiritual gifts in the church today."

**Dr. C. Ray Gentry**
Associational Mission Strategist
Southside Baptist Network

"I hadn't gotten far in my reading of *Dance of the Gifts* before the Spirit clearly brought to mind a church situation I was involved in and how the Fourth Foundational Principle could be used to bring vital insight. I wasn't disappointed. The further I journeyed in the book the more helpful "tools" I discovered. May you enjoy the same."

**Glen Schrieber**
Superintendent, EFCA Southeast

"Mark and Ken write a compelling book that reminds us that even the tensions and common challenges of church life often becomes a way that God brings out the various gifts of his people and uses them for his glory and purposes. I love the image portrayed in the book of leaders struggling to make decisions, wrestling even over the tension of points of views, but all are determined to not rest till God's will becomes clear. When there is this kind of *resonance* and *dance* you discover the beautiful way God works through the diversity of gifts. Church leaders are not robots, but real people who face real and raw decisions, but who can celebrate in the end how this amazing, sovereign God really does do what he does through us. It brings Him more glory that way."

**Mitch Schultz**
Founder, Fruitful Vine Ministries
Author of the Andre Michael Lansing series of novels

"From many years of experience in assisting troubled churches Mark Barnard and Ken Quick have given the church world even more keys to making that which is wrong right. *The Dance of the Gifts* is itself a gift to the church and its leaders. I read the whole thing and said, "Ouch!" several times. Pastors and church leaders shouldn't just read *The Dance of the Gifts* they should study it together. After which, the book should be taught to their church so that the principles of it are embedded into their corporate culture. As I have done with many other principles elucidated by Barnard and Quick, I resolved to put the principles of *The Dance of the Gifts* into my ministry experience and teaching emphasis."

**Peter A Joudry**
CEO, The Nehemiah Project

# Dedication

To our friends in Canadian Church of God Ministries who are seeking to tune their ministries to the Holy Spirit's leading.

"Has it ever occurred to you that one hundred pianos all tuned to the same fork are automatically tuned to each other? They are of one accord by being tuned, not to each other, but to another standard to which each one must individually bow."
- A. W. Tozer

# Table of Contents

# Foreword

In *Dance of the Gifts*, Mark Barnard and Ken Quick explore the interplay of spiritual gifts and the role of spiritual resonance as a way of hearing the voice of Jesus corporately. It provides a means for Christian leaders to walk in the confidence that the body has heard from Jesus.

These authors have a spiritual sensitivity that can identify "spiritual resonance." I have seen it displayed in consultation with local churches and over a broad network of churches. This sensitivity has been tested as well, through situations where little resonance existed. Their ability to rest, find peace, and have faith in the process and, more importantly, in Jesus, positioned them to wait calmly for resonance in the body to occur.

Blessing Point Ministries, which Mark and Ken lead, has walked with our network of churches over eighteen months to discern what Jesus is saying to our district. There were numerous times when the interplay of spiritual gifts resonated in such a way that it revealed what Jesus was saying to us as leaders for our body of believers. With their gracious guidance, we have heard clearly from Him and are now in the process of a long and ever-enduring obedience to Jesus.

I commend this book and the discipline of seeking corporate spiritual resonance to you. I encourage you to begin this exciting and challenging walk with the Lord of the Church.

Kenneth N. Wiedrick
Director of Ministry Services
Canadian Church of God Ministries

# Introduction

One day I (Mark) got stranded at the far end of a nearby lake. The propeller (and the nut that held it on) fell off my boat's electric motor. Fortunately, I had a backup prop on board. Smart! Unfortunately, I had nothing to secure it with. Dumb! All the fishhooks, wire leads, and bent safety pins I had couldn't secure the propeller to the motor. After hours of fitful (and prayerful) attempts to fix it, God sent a helpful park ranger to tow me back to the dock.

Leaders who are trying to discern God's will for their ministry can get stuck the same way, and all our attempts to extricate ourselves fall short. In *The Dance of the Gifts*, we will reflect on some truths that we hope may reconnect modern spiritual leaders with a biblical model of decision making. *The key question which will focus our efforts is: How do we—as a staff, a board, or a congregation—discern the voice of the Spirit when it comes to corporate decisions?*

Spiritual leaders find themselves looking for help with this all-important question, but they often run to the fishhooks and bent safety pins of secular authors and leadership gurus to help them. We borrow from the world's management and leadership libraries because we believe help can be found there. The wisdom we sometimes glean there reflects, if not biblical truth, at least biblical values, which justifies our borrowing from it. However, borrowing the world's decision-making mechanisms is the biblical equivalent of "leaning on a bent reed."

Os Guinness describes this "borrowing" tactic in his book, *The Call*:
> The same vast assembly of plans and procedures that
> we use to put an astronaut on the moon or market a
> new computer chip can also be mustered to 'grow a
> church' or 'evangelize an unreached people group.'

In short, the modern world quite literally 'manages' without God. We can do so much so well by ourselves that there is no need for God, even in His Church. Thus modern people can be profoundly secular in the midst of explicitly religious activities.[1]

In the church, we slip into "managing without God" subtly. It's not hard to confuse practical human wisdom with God's divine instructions. R.A. Torrey wrote in his book, *The Person and Work of the Holy Spirit*:

> The whole evangelical church recognizes theoretically at least the utter insufficiency of man's own righteousness. What it needs to be taught in the present hour, and what it needs to be made to feel, is the utter insufficiency of man's wisdom.[2]

What Torrey called "man's wisdom" we at Blessing Point Ministries call "mere-man thinking." We draw the phrase from Paul's rebuke of the Corinthians' groupie-like behavior around their favorite teachers, where he asks them *"Are you not carnal? Are you not walking like mere men?"* (1 Cor. 3:3) In other words, "You are acting like just like unsaved people, reflecting the attitudes of the world in your thinking, behavior and leadership. You should be *better* than that!"

Expedient, pragmatic, secular decision-making often hides under the guise of a "sanctifying" prayer at the start of a church board or business meeting. When it does, we are becoming "biblical," but it is not a part of the Bible for which we want to be known. The Apostle John recorded the words of Caiaphas' the High Priest as the

---

[1] Os Guinness, *The Call* (Nashville: Thomas Nelson, 1998) 149.
[2] R.A. Torrey, *The Person and Word of the Holy Spirit* (New York: Revell, 1910) 149.

Sanhedrin considered the unjust arrest of Jesus: *"You know nothing at all, nor do you take into account that it is expedient for you that one man die for the people, and that the whole nation not perish"* (John 11:49-50). Caiaphas did not realize he was speaking prophetically, nor did God allow his "expedient" decision to circumvent the glory of His will. Nonetheless, there was a price to pay for his pragmatic decision as there always is for churches which engage in expedient, "mere-man" thinking.

We hope and pray that the simple principles laid out in this book will resonate with you and summon you back to elements of our spiritual birthright. We have access to the "mind of Christ" through the Holy Spirit and the spiritual gifts He imparts (1 Cor. 2:16)! We believe that the Lord longs to be in the center of our thinking and decisions as ministry leaders, and to *abide* there. He reveals how through His Word, and though the process is simple, it is not easy. As you practice these principles, may they become the strong "cotter-pin" on the propeller of your ministry, never leaving you stranded or unsure of what to do next, and never needing to lean on the fish hooks and bent pins of secular leadership.

Rev. Mark R. Barnard
Dr. Kenneth Quick
January 2020

# Chapter 1

# Gift-Based Ministry Leadership

Sometimes solutions to difficult problems are right in front of us. Seeking a super-sticky glue, Dr. Spence Silver, a researcher at 3M, discovered a compound that failed to meet the "super-sticky" requirement. In fact, he felt the glue quite useless as it was easily removed from wherever it stuck. Later, another 3M researcher, Art Fry, had a problem. He sang in his church choir but the slips of paper he used as page markers kept falling out of his hymnal. Remembering Silver's not-so-sticky glue, Fry applied it to slips of paper which he then stuck to the pages of his hymnal without causing damage. Post-It Notes were thus born.

A gift-based approach to ministry leadership sits right in front of believing leaders—they all possess a piece of its puzzle. They don't have to go anywhere to see it or discover it. Yet it constitutes a significant paradigm shift for most ministry leadership models because history teaches us that the Church quickly and easily loses its grip on it. We at Blessing Point Ministries rediscovered it quite by accident as a part of our corporate healing process.

The process we facilitate involves gathering groups of church members at retreats to walk through their ministry's history to have "ears to hear what the Spirit is saying" to their church (Rev. 2-3). We always encouraged those gathered to yield themselves to the filling of the Spirit to discern His Voice. Over fifteen years of doing this in over 75 churches, we watched a powerful pattern emerge.

When sharing the painful events of their history, participants at the historical retreat viewed these moments through different spiritual "lenses" or perspectives. Over time, we began to identify the operation of the spiritual gifts Paul listed in Romans 12 and 1 Corinthians 12. The gathered body, often 50 to 150 people, would see and discuss the painful historical events through the multiplicity of their spiritual gifts.

A person with the gift of mercy might temper outrage over a leader's moral failure by reminding the group that "we are all prone to sin." One with the gift of encouragement might express the desire to address the situation clearly and courageously: "Let's do what Jesus tells us so we can put this trauma behind us and move on." A woman with the gift of discernment might sense underlying reasons for her church's historical problems: "There is something else; something we have been avoiding and we need to bring it to the light." A young adult with the gift of wisdom might call for repentance and reconciliation: "We need to do this *now* with each other, not wait until later."

We also saw that the different gifts (and their unique perspectives) were commonly at odds with each other. Tension would sometimes grow sharp between their perspectives. But as we persisted in focusing on what the Lord was saying to them, one gifted person would ultimately share an insight that struck a powerful *collective* chord. An immediate gasp of corporate recognition occurred. We witnessed this time after time. At that moment the gathered body experienced a *mutual, collective witness* of what the Spirit was saying to them. We as facilitators began to call that moment, "resonance."

As we went from ministry to ministry, working to heal congregations of various denominations, many with long-term patterns of dysfunction and pain, some even described by denominational leaders as "pastor-killer churches," the pattern described above reinforced itself on us and we began to trust it and watch for it. We were witnessing one of *God's ways*, a way He communicates with His people.

The gifted people differed from church to church, but the gifts they needed to hear from Him were all there. More importantly, we experienced that moment of *resonance* in each one, resulting in crucial corporate insight. The gathered body, by making their ears sensitive to hear what the Spirit was saying, hit exactly upon Jesus' message to them in their pain, and *everyone knew it!* His sheep had "heard His voice," an exclusive privilege for God's people under their Good Shepherd (John 10).

## The First Foundational Principle: Sovereign Guidance

The first principle behind this book is this: *God sovereignly guides believers with certain spiritual gifts to specific churches to help that ministry fulfill His unique purpose for them.* Everything needed to hear His heart is present in the gifted people He has sent to them. Wise leaders *believe* this and learn how to marshal these resources in the moments when they need them to discern and/or follow Christ's will for their ministry.

Let that statement sink in.

> *God sovereignly guides believers with certain spiritual gifts to specific churches to help a ministry fulfill His unique purpose for them.*

Normally we view the church we attend as one *we* selected, one which best meets our needs. Yet most believers pray the Lord guides them to the right church. Interview any group of church attenders and they will describe this experience. They tell of entering the church and *feeling at home, sensing the Spirit, loving the worship, feeling welcomed.* At that moment, they experience an internal confirmation that they received an answer to their prayers. This is the work of the Holy Spirit leading you to the "body" in which He desires you—and your gifts—to *serve* it and help it grow into the *"measure of the stature which belongs to the fullness of Christ"* (Eph. 4:12).

How we will serve there is not always at the center of our thoughts. Instead we focus on our theological, familial, relational and spiritual needs. However, serving that body is clearly what Jesus has in mind for every member of it. Ephesians 4:16 says, *"the whole body, being fitted and held together by what every joint supplies, according to the proper working of each individual part, causes the growth of the body for the building up of itself in love."*

What is a "joint" in the body of Christ? What does "every joint" supply? Every believer in a church body is a "joint," a hinge where muscles are attached, and movement and growth become possible. What we supply in that joint is the spiritual gift(s) God gave us. 1 Corinthians 12:7 says, *"But to each one is given the manifestation of the Spirit for the common good."*

## The Second Foundational Principle: Supernatural Resources

This leads us to the second foundational principle of this book: *Each one of the people under the umbrella of a ministry has supernatural resources available for the health and growth of our corporate body!*

As leaders, you also have such manifestations of the Spirit. God gives these gifts when we believe in His Son and receive salvation. The Spirit of God brings them when He comes to indwell us. Your gifts, mixed with your personality, are unique to you. Others may possess the same spiritual gift as you, but it manifests itself uniquely in each one. God doesn't like copies or clones. Each person may also have more than one gift, a "gift-mix." These equip us to fulfill our calling and our roles in the ministry of which we are a part.

These gifts of the Spirit vary in their expression. Some are public, others private. Some are more verbal, others "sensory." Some initiate action and some support it. Some are focused on the unsaved world and its needs, some on the believing body and its growth, some are individual-focused and some are group-focused. The various manifestations of the Spirit differ but they are designed to work together to *"cause the growth of the body for the building up of itself in love."*

Part of the process of spiritual growth entails the mature understanding and application of our spiritual gifts to the circumstances and contexts in which we find ourselves. There are times to share and times to keep quiet (1 Cor. 14:28, 30). Immaturity will not always recognize when to sit quietly and listen, or the significance of the truth: *The spirit of the prophets is subject to the prophets* (14:32). The Holy Spirit never *makes* us speak. Like love, He leaves that up to us.

## The Third Foundational Principle: Love

Paul makes it clear that utilizing our spiritual gifts, magnificent as they are, is not magic in terms of their impact. *Love is the lubricant that keeps all the body's gifts working together even when there is friction between the "joints."* Without love, even the mightiest gifts will be of little profit to the gifted one or to the body. That is why Paul begins the "Love Chapter" of 1 Corinthians 13 with the description of mega-manifestations of significant spiritual gifts:

> *If I speak with the tongues of men and of angels, but do not have love, I have become a noisy gong or a clanging cymbal. If I have the gift of prophecy, and know all mysteries and all knowledge; and if I have all faith, so as to remove mountains, but do not have*

*love, I am nothing. And if I give all my possessions to feed the poor, and if I surrender my body to be burned, but do not have love, it profits me nothing.* (13:1-3)

Paul describes possessing and using these gifts *in extremis*, but, minus love, they neither build up nor benefit the user. We need love and to be loving for our gift to fulfill us in its exercise. The Holy Spirit does not automatically provide love during their exercise. It is up to us to be filled with the Spirit and His fruit.

If you have learned to operate lovingly with your spiritual gifts, you've likewise learned how it energizes you. When we work in the realm of our giftedness and calling, we find ministry motivating and exciting. When we are called to work outside of our giftedness, we may be adequate (though sometimes not) but we are drained by the experience. Many times pastors and lay leaders have responsibilities that drain them, and too much work in ungifted areas can burn leaders out. If possible, we should "staff" our ministries around the giftedness of the individuals involved.

## The Fourth Foundational Principle: Tension

*Fourthly, we find ministry leaders sometimes unaware that God built natural tension between the spiritual gifts.* We should not be surprised by this if we understand what the gifts are: supernatural "manifestations" of His Divine attributes, the Father imparting a part of Himself, His "DNA", to us. The gift of prophecy expresses God's *justice*, and the gift of mercy His *compassion*. If two individuals with those gifts sit around a board table and deal with a moral violation by a member, they experience the natural strong tension between justice and mercy in God's own heart! God inducts us into this birthright experience.

True story: Once, as a part of a small group, the subject of divorce and remarriage came up. In the group there was a man with a strong prophetic gift. He was sensitive to God's commands and standards, and he forcefully made the point how divorce was contrary to God's blueprint for marriage and the church should not perform weddings for divorced individuals. "God *hates* divorce!" he exclaimed.

Also in the group was a woman known for an amazing gift of mercy, and she expressed—just as forcefully—that the church was a hospital, filled with broken people and sinners, and God forgave and cleansed those who took responsibility and repented if they had experienced a divorce. If they then found love, the church needed to support them, not drive them away. The discussion grew heated and tension mounted as the rest of the group looked on, becoming more and more anxious.

Finally, the leader held up his hands and said, "Hold on just a second! Which one of these is expressing God's heart right now?" Everyone took a mental step back and reflected on what they had heard, and someone then said, "I think *both* of them." And there was a gasp of resonance, a realization of what was just witnessed.

## Celebrate the Tension: It Reveals God's Heart

It is hard for leaders to get their heads around this kind of tension as a positive thing, but it is just the way God made our human bodies to work, so it should not surprise us to see the body of Christ working similarly. The tension created by opposing sets of muscles around our joints is what give our bodies strength and enables us to move.

This also means though that opposition or friction among gifted leaders in a ministry is the natural tension between different body "parts" expressing what God feels. Someone with the gift of faith who invites chaos by taking faith-based risks will not see things the same way as a risk-adverse church treasurer with the gift of administration! The stronger the gifts (and personalities), the higher the natural tensions. Leaders need maturity about this, and it is why spiritual maturity is a prerequisite for overseers in ministry.

This tension can feel uncomfortable, especially when sharp. A ministry that has experienced painful or destructive conflict in their past will fear it. But God wants us to feel it because *He does*, and the higher the tension, the stronger the body grows if they learn how to exercise with it. He built it into the way His "body" functions.

If leaders don't welcome this "healthy" tension, (along with the love, mutual submission, and accountability good leadership requires), we end up with *overdeveloped and underdeveloped body parts*, where just one person's gift or one kind of gift is given a voice in a ministry. This effectively shuts down the possibility of resonance and is both dangerous and unhealthy. Multiplied stories exist (many that make the news) to prove it. Paul describes this in 1 Corinthians 12:17: *"If the whole body were an eye, where would the hearing be? If the whole were hearing, where would the sense of smell be?"* God never intended one gift (or gifted person) to dominate and the others be silenced.

Therefore, tension between spiritual gifts is *healthy*, if we have ears to hear what the Spirit is saying *through* the tension. We are inside God's heart, feeling the polarity of feelings He feels. When we do it right, the tension becomes *godly*, a true "God-thing" and exactly the way God designed the body of Christ to work. If His love governs the relationships (which *should* mark us as Christians), it strengthens the body profoundly.

If leaders learn to listen to each other this way and recognize the gifts at work, we grow to appreciate the differing giftedness of each other and learn when to draw on them. We will turn to the prophetically gifted when we need a sense of God's boundaries and justice in a situation, and to the mercifully gifted when we need to know how His compassion calls us to respond to it.

In a perfect, sinless world, it's a beautiful thing; the Bride of Christ functions in loving unity, responding to movements and tensions in the heart of her Divine Head as it encounters different issues and challenges. However, as we too often see in our consulting, most leaders are clueless about how spiritual gifts interact and how the Spirit communicates through them.

We are not saying that *all* tension between church people is related to the gifts. Many Christians lack maturity, the filling of the Spirit, and the lubricant of Divine love in the way they interact with each other. We are all selfish and self-willed. None of us is immune to the lusts of the flesh or the eyes or the boastful pride of life. Plus, the Devil knows where our weaknesses are and tempts us accordingly. We all have a degree of relational dysfunction to overcome from growing up with a sin nature in a sin-cursed world that constantly mars our participation in the body of Christ. We wound other parts of the body who don't see things our way or who challenge our ideas.

All this works against "resonance," and overcoming it is part of our growth—personally and corporately—to "master" the predator that lurks just outside everyone's door (Gen. 4:7). That's why God intends the gifts and ministries of the body to work to bring us all *"to the unity of the faith, and of the knowledge of the Son of God, to a mature man, to the measure of the stature which belongs to the fullness of Christ."* (Eph. 4:13)

Therefore, we as ministry leaders and congregations need to raise our game in better understanding how God designed spiritual gifts to work *together*. In doing so, we gain a deeper knowledge of His ways, His heart, and how He communicates with us. We learn to celebrate and enjoy the differences between us, even when expressed most strongly. Those differences can save our bacon!

In addition to the four foundational principles outlined in this chapter, we explore a fifth one in the next chapter. It's one that we've touched on here but, due to its importance, we develop it throughout the rest of the book.

# Chapter 1 Discussion Questions:

1. How does the idea that God sovereignly guides believers with certain spiritual gifts to specific churches impact the way you view your ministry?

2. How might viewing your spiritual gifts as a divine resource for ministry change the way you see spiritual gifts?

3. What is the role of love in the expression of spiritual gifts?

4. How do you normally view tension with other believers who don't see things your way?

5. If God designed tension between spiritual gifts, how might that change the way we view some leadership conflicts?

6. What do you think of the idea that different spiritual gifts reflect different aspects of God's heart? How does that impact the way you see your spiritual gifts?

# Chapter 2

# Resonance and Spiritual Gifts

Two key things tie all spiritual gifts together. The first is their Source: *"But one and the same Spirit works all these things, distributing to each one individually just as He wills"* (1 Cor. 12:11). No matter what your gift is, the same Holy Spirit gave yours to you and other gifts to other people just as He willed.

The Scripture indicates that your spiritual gift comes personally from Christ through the Spirit to complement our salvation: *"But to each one of us grace was given according to the measure of Christ's gift. 'WHEN HE ASCENDED ON HIGH, HE LED CAPTIVE A HOST OF CAPTIVES, AND HE GAVE GIFTS TO MEN.'"* The graciousness of our Savior is astonishing. We should be giving *Him* gifts for freeing us! Instead, He imparts them to us.

The distinction between the role of the Holy Spirit and the Lord Jesus in giving us gifts relates to our ministry calling. Paul tells us: *"Now there are varieties of gifts, but the same Spirit. And there are varieties of ministries, and the same Lord"* (1 Cor. 12:4-5). In other words, the Spirit provides differing gifts to people, who are then assigned differing *ministries* by the Lord Jesus. In giving these "ministers" different gifts, He equips them to do what He uniquely calls them to do.

All that God has done in Redemption is jaw-dropping, and hymn writers like Charles Wesley felt it: "Amazing love! How can it be that thou, my God, shouldst die for me?" How much more so when we consider that the One Who died for us now imparts and invests His attributes as gifts in us? He grants this that we might truly function as His hands and feet and voice, operating as a diverse yet unified whole. How solemnly, how carefully, and how humbly we should value and exercise these gifts from our Lord!

*Operation* is the second thing that ties spiritual gifts together. This is where both the tension and resonance occur. Today gifts get associated with events like birthdays and Christmas. But, like gifts we give to our children, many instruct that "Some assembly is required" or "Batteries are not included." The beauty of spiritual gifts is that we don't need to assemble them or supply a power source for them to operate. The Holy Spirit animates the gifts, energizes their expression, and supplies the empowerment as we walk with Him. The Bible thus calls spiritual gifts "the manifestation of the Spirit" (1 Cor. 12:7). We manifest and experience the operation of the Spirit when we use His gifts.

Your spiritual gift is a manifestation of one of God's attributes, through you and your unique personality. The same Holy Spirit operates through others with different spiritual gifts through their unique personalities. This becomes challenging when another gifted believer is passionate about an issue different from the passion your spiritual gift gives you. We fail to realize the *additional gift* God gives us at this moment: *an invitation into the tensions within His own great heart*! But how do we mere mortals recognize the Lord's leading when varying gifts view the same issue with passionate differences? How do we hear what the Spirit is saying to a church when the tensions run that high? Learning about something we call "spiritual resonance" becomes crucial.

## The Fifth Foundational Principle: Spiritual Resonance

*When we listen for the Voice of Christ corporately, through the input (and tensions) of what our combined spiritual gifts provide, we bear witness that there comes a moment when someone shares an insight or declaration that resonates with all the gifts in all the hearts.* The dictionary defines "resonance" as "the quality in a sound of being deep, full, and reverberating." This "reverberation" operates collectively across a gathered body, and the "same Spirit" gives us all "ears to hear" Him at the same time. It is a collective affirmation or recognition that the Body has just heard from the Lord.

We all experience this "inner witness of the Spirit" as believers, validated by Scripture. Romans 8:16 says, *"The Spirit testifies with our spirit that we are children of God."* This describes a *subjective* inner confirmation of an *objective* truth. The Holy Spirit "testifies" this truth to our "spirit" subjectively, confirming, sealing, and assuring us that we are God's children.[3] Corporate spiritual resonance is like this as well.

Sometimes the witness of the Spirit appropriately comes through a passage of "God-breathed" Scripture, the "Breath/Spirit of God" now breathes its life into us, speaking with power to our conscience. John Calvin, speaking of Romans 8:16, put it this way: "For when the Spirit testifies to us, that we are the children of God, he at the same time pours into our hearts such confidence, that we venture to call God our Father." In other words, it *completely* changes our perspective, producing a paradigm shift in our belief system. Again, this mirrors what we see in corporate spiritual resonance.

This inner confirmation of the Spirit occurs frequently in the lives of believers as they grow in their faith and knowledge of the Lord. They learn to recognize His Voice and sense His promptings. He

---

[3] Martyn Lloyd-Jones, *Joy Unspeakable* (Wheaton: Harold Shaw, 1984) 71.

guides, motivates, and convicts us as we go through life depending on Him. We seek that inner resonance between the Holy Spirit and our spirit to confirm that we are on the same page with Him.

Can we get such "inner testimony" wrong? This is where understanding spiritual resonance becomes important. Explaining a little of our consulting process can help. When we gather a church to walk through their history to hear what the Spirit is saying, we encourage them all to prepare their hearts for the experience. Hearing the Spirit speak is not an accident; it requires prayer and a rudimentary understanding of the way the Spirit works in us. The first key is yield oneself to the Spirit and the second is to be "filled" with the Spirit. They are two sides of the same coin.

Yielding to the Spirit is a matter of control. We put ourselves in the Spirit's hands to be used as He sees fit. This action connects to our spiritual gifts, for the Spirit will most often use us for what He has gifted us to do. If there are attributes of God the ministry needs exercised or understood in order to discern what God thinks and feels about our circumstances, each believer gains a piece of that supernatural enablement by yielding ourselves to Him. And we receive "ears to hear" what He is saying.

Being "filled with the Spirit" (Eph. 5:18) is also connected to control, but with *visible effects* like being "drunk with wine," its dissipating alternative. We, as Christians and churches, are now the "Temple of God", His dwelling place both individually (1 Cor. 6:19) and collectively (Eph. 2:19-22). When we have prepared our hearts, His Spirit can "fill" us as His Presence used to fill the Old Testament Temple and Tabernacle. God manifests His Presence within us, and we experience its unique power in spiritual resonance.

At Blessing Point, ministries call us when they experience ongoing corporate pain (i.e. splits, an exodus of people, moral failures of leadership, destructive conflicts, diminishing resources, etc.), and they have exhausted their own attempts at healing it. We gather a church or ministry on a Friday night and Saturday to seek God's input on and evaluation of their corporate spiritual journey. Because of the painful events, everyone's heart is tender and very anxious about what they fear will occur, that we will be digging up (and reminding them of) the ugliness of their past to no good purpose.

We prepare them by telling them "This is a spiritual event which requires spiritual preparation of your hearts before, and being filled by the Spirit during, our meeting." We give them guidelines for prayer beforehand. If congregations take it seriously (and most do at that point), then they are ready for the experience of what God made local churches to be, the "dwelling place of God in the Spirit" (Eph. 2:22). They together hear His voice through their gifts, and the impact is "resonance."

In that moment of resonance between the gifts of the Spirit and the Spirit Himself, a transformation occurs. Those gifts (and attributes of God) which are in natural tension move to *unity*, not fake unity, but a powerful, "We-just-heard-from-our-God! Wow!!" kind of unity. Confusion, uncertainty and anxiety melt away. They vanish in the assurance that they just heard from the Spirit of God with "ears to hear."

During the retreat, there are times when someone will feel they received a prompting or insight of the Spirit about an event, and they speak it out. What occurs at that moment is crucial for us as leaders to discern. The gathered body does not respond with assent to what they heard. *There is no resonance!* The second thing we help churches learn is that this too is a part of the biblical process of discerning truth. Paul says in 1 Corinthians 14:29-33:

> *Let two or three prophets speak, and let the others*
> *pass judgment. But if a revelation is made to another*

*who is seated, the first one must keep silent. For you can all prophesy one by one, so that all may learn and all may be exhorted; and the spirits of prophets are subject to prophets; for God is not a God of confusion but of peace, as in all the churches of the saints.*

What is *most* remarkable about this remarkable passage is the "judgment passed" on what a prophet is prompted to speak. New Testament "prophecy" is different than Old Testament prophecy. Just because a prophet says passionately, "I believe the Lord is saying _____ to us!" does not mean they are hearing from God. We joke in our consults that, if someone feels the Spirit is prompting them to speak, and they do, but there is no resonance, it was not the Spirit of God but last night's pepperoni pizza prompting them. The body receives *resonance* if the prophet speaks from the Spirit. This is how "judgment" is passed.

Another important piece here is how the *right* to speak is affirmed. If someone else who has not spoken feels the Spirit prompt them, the person who is speaking is to sit down and be quiet! Paul says this is so *"all may learn and all may be exhorted."* He recognized that sometimes we need to hear from different people to receive a message. If we just hear one person, their sensitivities may not be attuned to our own.

We sometimes hear people say, "I *must* keep speaking because the Spirit is upon me!" But Paul gives another key principle about how gifts work: *"The spirits of the prophets is subject to the prophets."* In other words, the Spirit never *forces* anyone to do or say anything! In fact, just the opposite should occur. Someone speaking should always show deference to another who feels God has spoken to them. Everyone else either resonates, saying "Yes! That was God", or there is no resonance and you keep going.

## If Only

When we see this moment of resonance as consultants and feel its effects on a congregation, it breaks our hearts. Most never experience it, especially in the places (board rooms, business meetings) and times (conflict, controversy, doctrinal question, moral failure) when it is most needed! In the Upper Room Discourse, Jesus describes this experience as the "Spirit of truth guiding us into all the truth":

> *But when He, the Spirit of truth, comes, He will guide you into all the truth; for He will not speak on His own initiative, but whatever He hears, He will speak; and He will disclose to you what is to come. He will glorify Me, for He will take of Mine and will disclose it to you. All things that the Father has are Mine; therefore I said that He takes of Mine and will disclose it to you.* (John 16:13-15)

We believe this has a narrow meaning at the apostolic level when the Apostles received the "revelation" of the New Testament. But it also has a "church-level" experience demonstrated by the seven letters of Revelation 2-3. The Lord Jesus gives a Divine invitation at the end of each letter to "hear what the Spirit *says* (not "said") to the churches."

If only leaders in modern ministries, seeking both to maintain the unity of their body and to accomplish their Divine commission, used this indispensable equipment! God gives them *all they need* in the gifts the Spirit provides to the whole body! Our lament deepens as we receive calls from churches suffering corporate dysfunction due to its absence.

## Filling the Void with Other "spirits"

Ignorant of the "how-to" for a more biblical decision-making process, ministries fill the void with leadership principles from secular sources, usually from the current "leadership gurus", or successful business folk, or courageous military leaders. They assume that these successful models in other contexts can be applied to make their "ministry organization" better and more effective.

This pragmatism is so commonplace that our criticism of it brings reactions from some leaders. They consider us "narrow" or "naïve." "All truth is God's truth" we are told, an apparent validation of these secular constructs. However, failing to filter these secular models through a biblical grid, denominational leaders, pastors, and lay leaders absorb and apply the world's decision-making mechanisms. However, seldom does the meek ever inherit the earth in them! In few are the last first and the first last. And in few do the "unseemly members" possess a greater glory! But we witness *exactly* those principles at work when churches and leaders are trained to seek resonance.

Pastors, especially of larger churches, often see themselves as CEOs or army generals. Their gifts and their vision are exalted while most others are silenced, creating insecurity and a spiritual "caste system" among the not-so-gifted. It can foster a corrupting form of entitlement (and isolation) among the "highly gifted." Sadly, reports multiply of the moral wreckage caused by such pedestals.

There are important reasons why God did not design His churches to operate this secular way. He desired to empower *each and every Christian* with a unique contribution of one of His attributes to bless and energize His churches. The gifts also bless and energize the believer who contributes them. If you are in a ministry where you use your gifts regularly, you know how this works. It *motivates* you when you work in the realm of your gift. You may grow weary *in* the ministry, but never *of* the ministry.

## Learning about (and Discerning) Spiritual Gifts at Work

Many books, questionnaires, and seminars have been produced to help believers discover and define their spiritual gift(s). However, little has been written (that we have discovered) on the interplay *between* spiritual gifts and how they inform and guide a local body of believers. The preeminent goal of ministry leadership should be to have one's flock become more "Christ-minded" and "Spirit-energized." To do that, we must ascertain how Jesus speaks to and through the spiritual gifts He has sovereignly placed in our flocks.

The Apostle Peter gives a broad outline of the supernatural power which operates though the gifts when he says:

> *Whoever speaks, is to do so as one who is speaking the utterances of God; whoever serves is to do so as one who is serving by the strength which God supplies; so that in all things God may be glorified through Jesus Christ, to whom belongs the glory and dominion forever and ever. Amen* (1 Pet. 4:11).

"Speaking" and "service" form a powerful tandem, combining truth spoken with truth in action. Peter says that those who speak like this should present "the utterances of God." God's messages have different purposes, sometimes encouraging, rebuking, or seeking justice, sometimes teaching, or providing wisdom or discernment.

Those who "serve" use their gift, their "piece" of their Father's Divine attributes, to help the body demonstrate His goodness through the enablement provided by the Holy Spirit. Sometimes they show mercy or compassion, they provide timely, practical help; they exercise faith, or leadership, or bring order to chaotic situations. The gifts that don't involve speaking still communicate very loudly!

The following chart (Exhibit 1) shows the lists of spiritual gifts in New Testament passages. The shaded areas constitute communication/speaking gifts. The unshaded areas represent those that make up service-oriented gifts.

## Exhibit 1[4]

### New Testament Lists of Spiritual Gifts[5]

| 1 Cor. 12:8-11 | 1 Cor. 12:28 | Ro. 12:6-8 | Eph. 4:11 | 1 Pet. 4:11 |
|---|---|---|---|---|
| Word of wisdom | Apostles | Prophecy | Apostles | Speaking |
| Word of knowledge | Prophets | Service | Prophets | Service |
| Faith | Teachers | Teaching | Evangelists | |
| Gifts of healing | Workers of miracles | Exhortation/ Encouragement | Pastors | |
| Workings of miracles | Gifts of healing | Giving | Teachers | |
| Prophecy | Helps | Leadership | | |
| Distinguishing of spirits | Administration | Showing of mercy | | |
| Kinds of tongues | Kinds of tongues | | | |
| Interpretation of tongues | | | | |

---

[4] D.A. Carson, *Showing the Spirit* (Baker: Grand Rapids, 1987), 36. Emphasis ours.

[5] Missing from this list are two gifts commonly recognized as spiritual gifts; hospitality and intercession. While ample biblical evidence demonstrates the value of both traits, neither is specifically mentioned in the gift lists. But it is clear from the differences in the lists that they were not intended to be exhaustive, plus each gift has facets and dimensions that cause it to differ even from others with the same gift.

Some of the gifts have both a spoken and a service aspect. The gift of faith can be expressed verbally or through action. It communicates by example a divine message of the power of trusting God to the rest of the body. The gift of mercy communicates God's compassion, sometimes verbally but more often by demonstration and presence. The "working of miracles" gets as much space as gifts of "helps" and "service" though it is dramatically different. But sometimes we pray for a miracle when God knows all we need is someone with the gift of helps! Timely help carries a relieving message, God is faithful! In addition, helps, often viewed as one of the lesser gifts, mirrors the work of the Paraclete Himself who comes alongside to help in our time of need. One with the gift of giving will respond to calls from the gift of faith or helps. They become God's instrument to communicate He is still Jehovah Jireh. Nothing communicates God's love and power more practically than gifts of healing. What encouragement it provides when a congregation has one of its members healed from cancer or some other infirmity through gifts of healing or intercession.

Thus, all the gifts *communicate* a part of an overall Divine message, displaying the glory of some Divine attribute—God's mercy, grace, love, wisdom, justice, comfort, etc.—in a corporate context through a human instrument. Every believer active in fellowship or ministry has been touched by this at some point and probably at many points. But then, for some reason, we assume the Lord Jesus would *not* communicate similarly to a ministry in its decision-making processes, and we don't look for it. Learning to listen to Jesus at a corporate level, having *"ears to hear what the Spirit says to the churches,"* using the gifts He has placed in our congregation and around our boardroom tables, *we can gain the mind and perspective of Christ on every crucial ministry decision we face.*

## Overcoming Cultural Barriers to Hearing

How would we know when we have heard from the Spirit? The body (His sheep) *know* that Voice when we hear the chord struck by the Holy Spirit, the Giver of those gifts that expresses it. We are broken at this point because of our North American/Western cultural philosophy. The emphasis for too long has been on individualism and even on individuals with spiritual gifts. Gordon Fee writes, "Western Christians in particular are trained from birth to value the individual above the group, whereas in the New Testament perspective the community is still the primary reality, and the individual finds identity and meaning as part of the group."[6]

Our individualistic church culture renders us partially blind to the way Christ communicates to His churches. But we can adjust, overcome our North American fixation with independence and individualism. We can move toward the more biblical view of the deep connection, a true "one flesh" relationship God has created between believers in a ministry (Eph. 5:29-32). If we do, then we can begin to "discern the body" and the role of all the body's parts (that make the whole so much greater than their sum) and listen to the body's Head.

These experiences are our birthright as believers in Jesus. We want to delve into them more deeply in Chapter 3.

---

[6] Gordon D. Fee, *Listening to the Spirit in the Text* (Grand Rapids: Eerdmans, 2000) 124.

# Chapter 2 Discussion Questions

1. How do spiritual gifts demonstrate God's kindness toward his children?

2. Can you describe a time when you experienced resonance with what another gifted believer was sharing or doing?

3. Are your spiritual gifts more speaking or serving oriented, or some of both?

4. What are some dangers of adopting the world's decision-making practices in the church?

5. How has our cultural emphasis on individualism hindered our understanding of spiritual gifts?

6. How do spiritual gifts relate to ministry decisions when it comes to discerning the Spirit's Voice?

# Chapter 3

# The Role of Spiritual Gifts in Ministry

One way of stating the core question of our book is: *How does the Holy Spirit speak to a church/ministry?* Let no one misunderstand when we ask the question. We *firmly* believe and are *wholly* committed to the canon of the Scriptures, the Word of God, being the *only* infallible basis for our faith and practice. And we do not believe we can add or take away a jot or tittle from it.

However, we also believe, when a ministry experiences circumstances in which they need guidance and direction, *that spiritual gifts manifest and express the heart and mind of God to that body in those circumstances*. This manifestation will always, we repeat, *always* be in line with the Scriptures and never, ever contradict them! Additionally, He is not going to contradict Himself nor cease to be loving when He expresses Himself through the different gifts.

When we pose the above question to modern believers, the answers come slowly and with uncertainty. They usually stammer the answer in the form of a question: "Through the pastor?" "Through the congregation?" Through the elders?" "Through the Word of God?" They expose their "doctrine of the church" (ecclesiology) by their answers. Their awkwardness also betrays how rarely leaders/believers stop to consider this crucial question.

Their answers *all* have a degree of validity, but they overlook the *main* method God uses to communicate with His churches corporately: the interplay of the spiritual gifts—His attributes distributed to His children, the display of His "DNA" in us through the Holy Spirit. God provides this to each ministry. Jesus focused each of the Seven Churches in Revelation 2-3 on this methodology: *"He who has ears to hear, let him hear what the Spirit says to the churches"* (Rev. 2:7, 11, 17, 29; 3:6, 13, 22).

Note the present tense, *"what the Spirit says"* not *"said"* in these verses. Jesus calls on each local church to hear what the Spirit is *presently* saying to them. Revelation 2-3 are models of how the Lord of the Church now communicates about the things going on in their/our midst![7] In our consulting we've learned to recognize His unique message to a ministry when it resonates with *all* the spiritual gifts represented within a gathered body of believers who have come to listen.

This process works in micro and macro scenarios, at board and staff meetings, and at congregational meetings where major decisions are made. It also works in the toughest, most conflictual and painful situations (which is when we most often do our consulting). God supplies all the spiritual gifts needed "for the common good" within your ministry. But it also reveals the importance of discerning the different spiritual gifts God places in your ministry when they are operating because everyone should feel and value the contribution they are making to the ministry's "common good." There are many gift inventories available to help you and your people identify your spiritual gifts, however, you don't need to wait (or pay) to take a survey to discover or utilize your body's giftedness.

---

[7] For more on how The Seven Letters to the Churches function as models of divine corporate communication see *The Eighth Letter: Jesus Still Speaks! What is He Saying to Your Church?* By Mark Barnard and Ken Quick.

## Becoming Fellow-Workers with God

A former pastor once explained the best way to recognize one's spiritual gift: *"Your spiritual gift is the thing you do with the least amount of effort and the most amount of satisfaction."* When we operate "in the realm of our gift," it feels effortless and we feel energized. In ministry we will see, and often hear, that God operated through us and people felt the impact. Paul puts this in a strange but important way in 1 Corinthians 12:6: *"There are varieties of effects, but the same God who works all things in all persons."* In other words, we will all *see* different results, *feel* different effects as our gifts operate, but we will *sense* God's working in each one.

Paul describes this unique partnership with God when the gift operates: *"What then is Apollos? And what is Paul? Servants through whom you believed, even as the Lord gave opportunity to each one. I planted, Apollos watered, but God was causing the growth . . . For we are God's fellow workers; you are God's field, God's building"* (1 Cor. 3:5-6, 9). We become instruments God uses to accomplish His purposes. Even with our gifts working, we cannot make anything happen. That is up to God, but He invites us to be participants with Him in His "fields" and "buildings." We provide the material through our gift(s)—the words and the work, the "utterances" and the "service,"—that He uses for the "effects" He desires.

He does not *need* us, and we mess up far more than we should. Paul describes the "wood, hay and stubble" with which we often try to build up His Temple (1 Cor. 3:12, 15). But we are children He is training to operate in step with Him. He will also reward us for our labor in ways we can only imagine.[8]

---

[8] Ken has written a book on this called *Living for the Kingdom: Eternal Significance as Motivation for the Christian Life,* available digitally on Logos at

When we use our spiritual gifts, there is a sense then in which we are "along for the ride." That does not mean we can mentally or emotionally "check out." On the contrary, we must be engaged and in *control* of it. Again, Paul puts it succinctly: *"The spirits of prophets are subject to prophets"* (1 Cor. 14:32). He could have said this about any gift, but prophets are the most susceptible to feeling they are *compelled to* speak and don't have control over the compulsion. That is not the way God made it. Paul explains that God will not make things confusing, but peaceful and orderly, so no one can say "The Spirit *made* me do it."

That means we can choose to shut down or suppress our gift's expression, perhaps grieving or quenching the Spirit in the process. In every circumstance we can weigh if it is appropriate to exercise our gift, to speak or act. The use of one's gift should be submitted to the Spirit's leadership and filling, especially in "body" contexts where God gave it to edify and guide. We should exercise it in in a spiritually responsible way, following the Spirit's lead, being careful not to "quench" the expression of any gift by devaluing or rejecting it.

Because the gifts are spiritual in nature, the Holy Spirit actuates them within us. When operating in the sphere of our gift, it feels effortless because we're not forcing anything. This is a total God-thing, our Father in Heaven imparting a portion of His attributes to His children to build them up and make their ministry a full partnership with Him! You don't think about how you are speaking/acting/behaving as the Lord uses you. You become His instrument and sense a freedom and joyful satisfaction because Christ operates in and through you. We become conscious that

https://www.logos.com/product/25966/living-for-the-kingdom-eternal-significance-as-motivation-for-the-christian-life human inspiration and effort could not accomplish what we are doing.

## God's Pleasure and Our Own

Being a "fellow-worker" with the Trinity is deeply satisfying. It highlights how much God esteems us as His children. It is one thing to be God's child through no merit of our own, but it's quite another to realize God loves us enough to impart so precious a gift and to use us in the unfolding of His divine plan. Let that sink in. He believes in *you* so much that He makes this fabulous investment in you. Much of the blessing we receive is *God's pleasure* in working through us as we allow His Spirit to function by means of our gifts.

Therefore, the principle of "least amount of effort–most amount of satisfaction" can help individuals in your community of believers recognize their gifts. The gift of hospitality means Lisa loves to serve others and her non-anxious nature makes others feel at ease in her home. The gift of service or helps means Jim relishes mowing the church lawn or fixing things in the worship facility. The gift of leadership means Peggy clearly sees how to get her ministry from point "A" to point "B" as quickly as possible. The gift of pastor/teacher means Dale wants to communicate truth and see people grow, and to be patient while they do so.

The supernatural nature of the gifts is also demonstrated in the *timeliness* of their exercise. The Spirit knows when and where and with whom they are needed. Paul again tells us: *"There are a variety of gifts but the same Spirit. There are a variety of ministries but the same Lord"* (1 Cor. 12:4-5). The Spirit's gifting and the Lord's ministry calling will differ for each person. Jesus assigns a ministry that funnels your gifts in a specific direction and time. One's ministry calling serves His eternal purposes.

This "variety of ministries" impacts the shape and burden of your church body. Four different people in your church may have the gift of evangelism. Jim preaches the gospel on street corners, burdened by the lostness of the mass of humanity in the city. Matt serves in a campus ministry, burdened to reach lost college students with the gospel. Todd's heart was burdened by the need in Africa, called to work in Uganda as a church planter. Hazel gently exercises her gift as a hospice nurse, burdened to reach frightened people shortly facing death. The difference is not one of gifting but of ministry calling. All express the Father's heart in reaching lost sheep, but the variety in them is vast.

## Gifts Vary in Their Degree, but Not Value

History has been shaped by those who possess strong spiritual gifts and callings. Saint Augustine, the gifted thinker and teacher, shaped Christian thought for centuries and still does. The gifts of Calvin, Luther, the Wesley brothers, Spurgeon, D.L. Moody, Mary Slessor, Amy Carmichael, and Billy Graham have transformed church history because of their unique gifts and callings.

But there were always *other* gifted people behind the scenes whom God used to impact those lives, like the Sunday School teacher, Mr. Kimball, who prayed for and pursued the young shoe salesman, D. L. Moody, with the gospel. Plus, none of these luminaries would have had the impact they did unless surrounded by people with gifts of administration, giving, or wisdom. The names of these "lesser lights" will be rewarded in heaven but never make front page news.

The difference in the strength of our gifting can be a divisive issue. Ambition and competition are dangerous, even in churches. The twelve apostles and New Testament churches had their challenges with both. The Apostle Paul had to set things straight about this: *"For through the grace given to me I say to everyone among you not to think more highly of himself than he ought to think; but to think so as to have sound judgment, as God has allotted to each a measure of faith"* (Rom. 12:3).

Paul realized that his gifts and calling were expressions of God's grace to him. They were not related to the grades he got sitting under Gamaliel or the fact that he was discipled by Barnabas. Paul knew that ministry flowed from his gifts and calling, not his efforts. He just put himself in the place where God could use him and kept moving. We too should recognize that, whatever gifts and calling we receive, it had nothing to do with our efforts. Like salvation by grace through faith (Eph. 2:8-9), we have been *"created in Christ Jesus for good works, which God prepared beforehand that we should walk in them"* (Eph. 2:10).

If we struggle with poor self-esteem, in our immaturity we might dream that we will be the next Billy Graham or Nancy DeMoss Wolgemuth! But God breaks molds. Only one person has the gifts and calling of Billy Graham or Nancy DeMoss Wolgemuth. When Jesus' caught his disciples discussing who among them was the greatest, they grew quietly ashamed as He set a child before them to illustrate the humility they lacked. It may be hard to admit we struggle with covetousness at that level (Mark 9:33-34). The reality is two people may have the same spiritual gift and not have it to the same degree or effect.

The parable of the talents indicates that individuals are granted differing capacities of giftedness (Matt. 25:14-18).

> *For it is just like a man about to go on a journey, who called his own slaves and entrusted his possessions to them. To one he gave five talents, to another, two, and to another, one, **each according to his own ability**; and he went on his journey. Immediately the one who had received the five talents went and traded with them, and gained five*

*more talents. In the same manner the one who had received the two talents gained two more. But he who received the one talent went away, and dug a hole in the ground and hid his master's money* (Emphasis ours).

Just as there were five talent, two talent, and one talent people in Jesus time, we need to recognize the upper limit on our own abilities and gifts. Our purpose is to be faithful to follow the Lord with the gifts He grants us in the ministry environment He places us.

## Your Ministry's "Gift Capacity" and God's Purpose

The principle that God places *people* with certain gifts in a church to help it accomplish its unique purpose can be raised up a level. He does the same with where He places *churches*. Just as there are different human bodies, some athletic, some intellectual, some burley and some slender, God made each church to do unique work in the place He plants it. When we seek to copy other successful ministries, we may miss the unique strengths God gave us. Each ministry has its own sovereignly assigned *gift capacity*, which grows or diminishes depending upon the faithfulness and wisdom of its leadership.

How does that relate to your ministry's capacity for ministry? It is helpful to understand mega-churches in this context. How did they get to be so large? Are they all built on the personalities of flashy pastors? Hopefully not or they stand on a sandy, shaky foundation (and, sadly, we have seen that sand foundation result in the destruction of some).

A ministry's size, like that of the Jerusalem or Ephesian church in Acts, can be a direct result of the gifted people they possess. Greatly gifted pastors tend to attract greatly gifted lay people, and God uses these "human resources" to expand their gift capacity further. The degree of giftedness available results in an *obligation* to grow as people stay faithful and obedient! The ten talents *should* make ten talents more. Danger arises though when the "ten talent" pastors and churches become the model and set expectations for "one talent" or "five talent" pastors and churches. All the church-growth books in the world cannot accomplish the feat, any more than they could in the First Century. The church in Sardis was never going to be like the Ephesian Church, nor should it be.

It is interesting to watch God take gifted people from the Jerusalem mega-church and scatter them as a result of the persecution caused by the stoning of Stephen. Luke makes clear that the apostles stayed in Jerusalem (Acts 8:1), but he follows Philip and demonstrates how the Spirit uses this deacon's gifts to start ministries in Samaria and (probably) Ethiopia. Ananias in Damascus and Barnabas as well play a part in discipling the newly converted Saul of Tarsus.

Other factors play a part in why some churches grow large, like demographics, ethnicity, the community's spiritual history and receptivity, spiritual warfare, and the health of the church. At Blessing Point, we've consulted with enough large churches to know that size does not equate to health, any more than it does in a human body. However, the size of a church directly reflects the gift capacity God places in it. Why put so many gifted people in one church? That's ultimately His business. Ours is to remain faithful wherever He calls us to minister, and hope we are not burying His resources under rocks and not using them.

Whether your ministry is large or small, whether you are pastor, staff member, or lay leader, your responsibility in your ministry is the exact same: *maximize the effectiveness of your Sovereignly provided gift capacity!* This is what enables one, five, or ten talent believers to make more talents.

God leaves this up to us; He just gives us the resources and tells us to *"Do business until I return"* (Lk. 19:13). He sent us people He gifted that we might draw upon and maximize their giftedness. Unfortunately, many ministries just use the gifts of a few, not seeing their task as utilizing and maximizing *every muscle* in their ministry's body.

If you faithfully grow the gifted people you have, learning to draw on all their gifts, He will send higher capacity people to your church. They may come in the form of an unsaved "Saul of Tarsus" walking through your door looking for people to persecute. Be faithful and His larger purposes for the ministry will unfold as you learn the power of spiritual resonance with those gifted people.

# Chapter 3 Discussion Questions:

1. If the Spirit inspires the spiritual gifts, would those gifts ever contradict each other? Why or why not?

2. If the Holy Spirt inspired God's Word, and inspires the spiritual gifts, would a message from a gifted individual ever contradict the written Word of God? Why or why not?

3. What do you do for God that takes the least amount of effort but gives you the most amount of satisfaction?

4. What are some of the implications of the phase, "The spirits of prophets are subject to prophets (1 Cor. 14:32)?

5. What are some things you do to expand your gift capacity, to use your talents to make more talents?

6. How does realizing that ministries may have differing gift capacities change the way you view your ministry?

# Chapter 4

# Satisfied with Few Gifts

Many ministries grow "content/comfortable" with just a few people expressing its corporate giftedness. It is the equivalent of the servant who takes the "talent" and buries it. The other gifted people will abdicate their potential to the dominance of those few. They won't raise their hands and ask why the ministry isn't using them. Being content with a few "performers" doing most of the work, you become a "Steven Hawking" church—maybe breath-taking brilliance at the top, but the rest of the body withers.

We believe Jesus "births" each church; they are His beloved babies. He laid the burden to start the church in a certain location on the hearts of its founder(s). He assigns a mix of gifts in the church body designed to facilitate His unique purpose for them. He then adds to their number more gifted people as the ministry stays faithful and grows stronger. A ministry like this "glorifies God and enjoys Him" when they work as He intended. The spiritual gifts He gives are not an end unto themselves, the *mission* is. God gives exactly what/who is needed to fulfill His calling on their lives so that the church can fulfill its unique mission where He planted it.

## The Scriptures Provide the Model
The Scriptures provide a powerful picture of how God uses His gifted people. The sixty-six books of the Old and New Testaments were written by about thirty-five individuals over 1500 years. They came from varying backgrounds, lived (and wrote) in different

cultures and languages. These individuals had differing gifts as the Spirit used them, but unlike us, it does not appear that every Israelite received this blessing of a spiritual gift.

We can identify many of the gifts these writers had. There were leadership gifts, like Moses, Joshua and Nehemiah. Some were prophets, like Jeremiah, Ezekiel, and Daniel. Ezra's gift was more in line with that of pastor/teacher—he studied and taught. David, in addition to a strong leadership gift, also had the gift of faith given the risks he took. Solomon had a reputation for wisdom and his administrative gift facilitated the Temple's construction.

All this was a precursor. Most authors of the New Testament had apostolic gifts befitting their role, but a few did not. Luke, the author of his Gospel and Acts, was a physician who used his gift of service to Paul's benefit. James, the epistle writer, was not an apostle but was recognized as the wise pastor of the Jerusalem church (Acts 15).

All these individuals writing over fifteen hundred years, with differing gifts, ethnicities, cultures, experiences and contexts, yet with incredible, supernatural unity and consistency. This is the impact of the *same* Holy Spirit dwelling in them. 2 Timothy 3:15 tells us, *"All Scripture is inspired by God* [literally *God-breathed*] *and profitable for teaching, for reproof, for correction, for training in righteousness; so that the man of God may be adequate, equipped for every good work."* And Peter adds: *"For no prophecy was ever made by an act of human will, but men moved by the Holy Spirit spoke from God"* (2 Pet. 1:21).

God used their diversity of gifts to communicate His singular yet multi-faceted message to humankind. The principle "many gifts-same Spirit" operates when seeking what the Spirit says to a church. He will *never* contradict Himself. Digest this! He never has, through the vast time, personalities, and experiences represented by the biblical authors, and He will not now. This unity amidst vast diversity guides us in the use of the gifts in church life. Look once more at 1 Corinthians 12:3-12, and the principle of unity amidst the diversity of gifts crystalizes:

> *Now there are varieties of gifts, but the same Spirit. And there are varieties of ministries, and the same Lord. There are varieties of effects, but the same God who works all things in all persons. But to each one is given the manifestation of the Spirit for the common good. For to one is given the word of wisdom through the Spirit, and to another the word of knowledge according to the same Spirit; to another faith by the same Spirit, and to another gifts of healing by the one Spirit, and to another the effecting of miracles, and to another prophecy, and to another the distinguishing of spirits, to another various kinds of tongues, and to another the interpretation of tongues. But one and the same Spirit works all these things, distributing to each one individually just as He wills.*

The Trinity exercise Their unique roles in equipping us to use their attributes as a community of faith, imparting the variety of gifts, ministries and effects. But the purpose of this distributed diversity is unity! This is how He created the "body of Christ" to operate to accomplish His Kingdom purposes. Paul emphasizes the word "same" or "one" or "one and the same" Spirit throughout. Like a true human body, the diversity of the gifts and the ways the Lord assigns them to be used will have the same qualities of unity that the Scripture has.

## This Is How We Are Unique

Spiritual leaders need to fully grasp this. It is what makes us unique, unlike any other leadership context. The interplay of diverse spiritual gifts provides differing perspectives, even passions, on the same subject, problem or conflict. But if they share a common inspiration in the Holy Spirit and operate under His control, we can anticipate a unifying effect, the "resonance," when those gifts work together, and we hear what He seeks to say to the church. Inspired/filled by the same Holy Spirit, they should all be on the same wavelength . . . and *know it*.

Operating with spiritual sensitivity, people will recognize the Spirit working through the different believers with their differing gifts. As a result, they will listen to different parts of the body providing "attribute information" from the "Head" and know that's what they are hearing. It is a failure at just this point we see as consultants.

Do you know how to listen to all the gifts with all their (passionate and conflicting) perspectives that God placed in your church body? Do you know how to seek the "collective assent" (resonance) that tells the body they have just heard from the Lord? Are some parts of the body ignored because they are young (or old), impoverished, weak, homely, unsophisticated, or don't hold to the party line? You have just cut off a probable source of God's input through their gifts.

## Learning to Listen and Waiting Until You Hear

The Bible instructs us regularly to "wait on the Lord." Why is that? Because leaders face temptations to act on their own authority and understanding rather than on God's. Saul did this, not waiting for Samuel before he took matters into his own hands (1 Samuel 13). It became a pattern for him that cost him his leadership, demonstrating how serious it is. Much of Saul's sin had to do with an unwillingness to *wait* and to *listen* before acting.

Discerning what the Spirit is saying through the various gifts in your body takes more time to process than executive, unilateral decisions, but it is time well-spent and God-intended. He uses the process to teach important lessons in faith/trust related to His attributes. As a result, people get to know Him better and feel they have made a significant contribution.

Perhaps most important, they know that leaders are *listening* to them. This alone will repair much of what goes wrong with churches, between genders, with older and younger believers, and between cultures, races, and ethnicities. These should be the goal for any shepherd/leader. It is certainly God's goal and the way He wants His Church to look before a watching world. We have become too enamored with *church structure* (Congregational, Presbyterian, etc.) providing this rather than the Spirit.

When dealing with a sharp conflict, or a moral or doctrinal issue, it takes sensitivity to the Spirit (and a lot of love and patience) to discern the message that resonates with all the gifts. Expediency, power-trips, control, and haste all result in ill-fated decisions when facing such issues. The impact can be disastrous. Ask Joshua about the Gibeonites (Josh. 9), or Moses about striking the rock (Num. 20). That kind of reactive leadership does not reflect the kind of biblical decision-making process reflected in Paul's body analogy.

## The Dance of the Gifts

Certain gifts (or gifted people) can hog the limelight. The Bible warns us that, when this happens, it's like the whole body becomes an "eye" or an "ear" (or a "mouth") and the "less seemly gifts" get silenced (1 Cor. 12:17). If your church idolizes its pastor or its worship leader/team, or it has a fixation on one kind of ministry, this prevents it from valuing and listening to all the gifts God gave the body.

Like Ecclesiastes so wisely instructs us, to everything—and that includes every gift—there is a season. The danger comes when a set of gifted people decide theirs are the *only* gifts that matter. A leadership team made up of people who all have the gift of administration will have a very organized but extremely narrow ministry! Other gifts may give input, but the team decides if there isn't a well-organized plan offered, it is not helpful. There would be little room for the input of the other gifts that God has placed in your body. A wise leader wants people on his/her team who are *differently gifted.*

A controlling spirit among leaders or members will also derail hearing what the Spirit says to the church. We should not discount *any* gift from *any* believer. Paul reminded the Corinthians, *"the members of the body which seem to be weaker are necessary"* (1 Cor. 12:22). Leaders only learn to listen to such "necessary" gifts if they have contributed wisdom at a key moment. We have seen that God often hides His input in such folk to get this message across to leaders.

True story: We were consulting in a church with a decades-long history of painful conflict and distrust with its pastors. Part of our process is to walk a church through its history at a weekend retreat, empowering everyone present to use their gifts to listen to what Jesus is saying about these painful events and what His purpose was for them. We came to the key moment (we always do) where we heard about an event that formed a hinge moment that changed the direction of the church and broke trust in leadership. Wounded emotions ran high.

We know to slow down at those moments and help facilitate the body to listen to what Jesus is saying through their gifts. It takes a while for everyone to let go of their pain and listen, but soon they were all seeking to discern His message. It went on for maybe thirty minutes, and people were offering ideas: "I think Jesus is saying this . . ." or "I believe the Spirit is saying that . . ." But there was no resonance, no unified "That's it!" Their frustration mounted.

One thing we also encourage a church to do is bring their keen teenagers to the retreat as the teens will see the church operate the way Christ intended, probably for the first time. It will make sense to them. This church encouraged their teens to come and a number were present. As the adults struggled with what Christ was saying to them, a ninth-grade girl finally turned to her mom and whispered, "I think Jesus is saying this . . ." Her mom jumped to her feet and said, "My daughter is a little shy, but she heard Jesus saying . . ." Immediately, *everyone* in the room felt the weight of her words and there was an audible gasp of resonance and a sweeping, corporate sense of brokenness.

It was *just like Jesus* to give that message to one of the "least significant" of His children in the room (as adults reckon significance when it comes to leadership and guidance). And they also needed the dose of humility it provided. When they carefully listened (and kept listening) and let the Spirit use all their gifts, they saw their most painful events with Divine clarity. They went on from that moment to discern what Christ's message was for their church, taking courageous steps to make things right with people who had left the church, including former pastors and leaders (and their spouses) they had wounded.

Resonance does not mean an experience of *reverberation*, like sitting too close to the speakers at a concert. We have discovered that spiritual resonance entails a collective assent to an idea, concept, or truth occurring at the same moment across a room, with young/old, mature/immature, male/female, leader/participant all grasping it at the same moment. It impacts emotions simultaneously as well. We have seen large groups immediately break into tears. But, because we are talking about people indwelt by the Holy Spirit, it is *more* than just a common experience.

## Making Room for All the Gifts

Some spiritual gifts are quieter than others and often hold the key to resonance. My (Mark's) wife has the spiritual gift of wisdom. (And, yes, it is true that opposites attract!) I can explain a complicated church situation to her and, in the mysterious (to me) working of her gift, she unlocks the dilemma, usually in one quiet, matter-of-fact sentence. I am stunned every time she does this, though after thirty-five years of marriage I should be used to it! But she is a tranquil soul and dislikes speaking in public.

This is true in your ministry as well. Some gifts need encouragement to speak up, some do not. Rarely will the gift of wisdom contribute to a discussion without being asked. The gift of discernment likewise stays quiet if it "discerns" its advice will fall on deaf ears. It stuns us to see the lack of understanding most spiritual leaders possess of these dynamics, and they fail to wait on the Lord and listen for them.

Is your church safe enough, loving enough, for all the gifts to operate and wise enough to ensure that they all get heard? If there isn't love, you hear only a clanging gong. If it has become unsafe, you grieve the Holy Spirit Who gives those gifts to help you know the mind of Christ. Leaders may be reading books on management and leadership, taking retreats to sharpen their acumen, but be overlooking the most significant resource the Spirit provides to help them. What is the Spirit saying to your church through *all* the gifts? It is not a message that "might" or "power" will provide (Zech. 4:6).

The Holy Spirit speaks to the *group* and confirms the communal message by an internal witness. Everyone expresses the hearing of His Voice in some way. As He speaks to our spirits that we are the sons and daughters of God, this "resonance" is tuned to the same "pitch." It can occur in any group setting of believers: an elder board meeting or congregational business meeting or women's retreat, etc.

A Spirit-anointed message strikes a "resonate chord" with those assembled, and they feel it *simultaneously*. We believe this experience is rare today because of the cultural focus on individualism and a lack of "discernment of the body".

## The Body and Bride as Illustrations

God has given us many illustrations of how He intends things to work. Paul's body analogy helps us here so let's return to it. How does "the body" of Christ stay on the same page as its Divine "Head?" When we think of the "head" of our churches, we assume it to be humans entrusted with leadership over us. It may be called a Session, Deacons, Elders, Leadership Team, Pastoral Staff, or Church Board. But God intended that these "heads" ultimately be subordinate to their True Head, and that is Jesus. It is *His* church by right of redemption, and He does not share ownership. Rather He entrusts it as a stewardship to under-shepherds who will one day give an account (Heb. 13:17).

So, under whichever ecclesiastical structure or title you function, those roles make up only *its subordinate "head."* Paul gives us a second image in Ephesians 5 to clarify the role we are in as leaders, that of a *bride* whose Divine Husband loves and gave Himself in sacrifice to redeem her and now works to sanctify her completely (Eph.5:21-32). In this Divine/human union, the "marriage partners" have headship/submission roles. They possess differing sets of responsibilities in these roles. We are Christ's "body" only through His indwelling Spirit, even as a husband and wife are joined to become "one flesh," which the apostle admits is a "great mystery."

It is crucial as leaders to get our minds and hearts around the reality that Jesus is in the role of husband and "Head" of the "one flesh" partnership with His Bride. She has her own "head" (whatever the ecclesiastical structure) but is submissive to His Headship because He *always* indwells her. *That* is the role of church leadership. They haven't been left alone to figure out what to do or how God sees what's going on. They are accountable to hear from *their* Head and follow His input. Their role responsibility is to interface with Divine leadership through prayer and the Word of God (Acts 6:4). When they are uncertain what to do or are in conflict/tension over a decision or face a moral dilemma or the need for church discipline, they should call the body together and use all the spiritual gifts God has given the body to hear what the Spirit is saying.

We cycle back around to the admitted fact that many congregational "heads" have lost touch with *the* Head. Instead, these groups lean on their own understanding and operate on purely human leadership principles. It is nothing new, and the apostles spoke to the danger in the First Century as well. Paul wrote the Colossians because they had an influencer in their midst seducing them in that direction. He told them:

> *Let no one keep defrauding you of your prize by delighting in self-abasement and the worship of the angels, taking his stand on visions he has seen, inflated without cause by his fleshly mind, and not holding fast to the head, from whom the entire body, being supplied and held together by the joints and ligaments, grows with a growth which is from God* (Col. 2:18-19).

John also describes a controlling leader named Diotrephes, of whom he says:

> *I wrote something to the church; but Diotrephes, who loves to be first among them, does not accept what we say. For this reason, if I come, I will call attention to his deeds which he does, unjustly accusing us with wicked words; and not satisfied with this, he himself does not receive the brethren, either, and he forbids*

*those who desire to do so and puts them out of the*
*church* (3 Jn. 9-10).

How fascinating and instructive that these leaders lost touch with
the Divine Head with ideas *"inflated without cause"* by their fleshly
minds. In other words, their head (and the ideas in it) got unspiritual
and it took their leadership the wrong direction.

## The Human Brain as an Illustration

Advances in medicine allow us to understand better how a body and
brain works together. The human brain is divided into two
hemispheres, and beyond that into various other structures: the
amygdala, thalamus, hypothalamus and pituitary. They interact and
function together (though differently) to regulate the body in a
healthy way. Spiritual gifts on a board or staff do the exact same for
the body of Christ. Each ministry leader serving on your leadership
team has been given gifts and a ministry to have the effect on the
body that God desires, sovereignly placed there for just the time you
are in.

Therefore, we believe a plurality of leaders are crucial to ministry
leadership and its decision-making. Even God operated this way
(Gen. 1:26!). It becomes dangerous to empower one person to make
all the decisions, no matter how much easier it is administratively or
how big the body gets. Each leader comes with sensitivities, gifts
and empathy level, as well as sinful habits and levels of brokenness.
Therefore, the Scriptures tell us not to lay hands on anyone "too
quickly" (1 Tim. 5:22) lest we share in responsibility for the sins
they commit as leaders.

Recent medical studies describe the brain and nervous system as
being more "liquid" in the way it fills us rather than hard-wired as
we usually conceive it. Edwin Friedman says in his book, *A Failure
of Nerve*:

"The brain turns out to function like a gland. It is the largest organ of secretion, communicating simultaneously with various parts of the body, both near and far, through the reciprocal transmission of substances known as neurotransmitters. In other words, the head is *present* in the body" [9] (Emphasis his).

The head's/brain's "presence" in the body performs a "shepherding" function, providing whatever hormones, vitamins, electrical impulses, etc. necessary for healthy operation. For a church's "head" to function well, they must be in touch with all the parts in their body. One person can't do this, not completely, because their gifts only make them sensitive to a "piece" of the whole picture the body represents. In our consulting, we regularly see the impact of church leaders separating/segregating themselves from the rest of the body with "us/them" attitudes. It breaks trust in their headship and leads to unhealthy bodies.

A local church is not "dancing by itself." It has a Divine Partner Who *must* lead and whom they *must* follow. "Resonance" is the communication *between* these dance partners as the Divine Partner leads. We are "one flesh/spirit" with Him, and He is "in us" through the indwelling Holy Spirit. When we move in harmony and in step with Him, we feel excitement and exhilaration! There is nothing quite like it. A congregation experiences unity and confidence in their human leaders when their decisions *resonate* with the Holy Spirit Who dwells in them. The head (leaders) receive positive feedback from the body they lead, because the Spirit's Presence resonates through it as they follow Him in the dance.

---

[9] Edwin H. Friedman, *A Failure of Nerve* (New York: Church Publishing, 2017) 18.

The connection between head/brain and body is a feedback loop. Friedman says again:

> "...neither brain nor body interacts with the environment alone, without the participation of the other. Thus, all the images that our brains collect are only obtainable through messages sent to the brain by our body's interactions with the environment. And, of course, how those data are then processed ultimately feeds back to affect our bodies."[10]

Watchman Nee describes the relationship between the mind of Christ and the body in a similar way:

> "All the members naturally possess a common feeling and that feeling expresses the mind of the body. And what is more, it is also the expression of the mind of the Head. Thus the mind of the Head is known through the body."[11]

R.A. Torrey, in *The Person and Work of the Holy Spirit*, describes the relationship between the Holy Spirit in the life of the church and in the life of the believer:

> "The Holy Spirit takes up His abode in the one who is born of the Spirit. The Apostle Paul said to the believers in Corinth in 1 Corinthians 3:16, 'Know ye not that ye are a temple of God, and that the Spirit of God dwelleth in you?' This passage refers not so much to the individual believer as to the whole body of believers, the church. The church as a body is indwelt by the Spirit of God. But in 1 Corinthians 6:19, we read, 'Know ye not that your body is the

---

[10] Ibid 131.
[11] Watchman Nee, *The Release of the Spirit* (Cloverland, IN: Sure Foundation Pub. 1965) 87.

temple of the Holy Ghost which is in you, which ye
have from God?"[12]

It is the relationship between these three "bodies"—the Lord of the Church, the local church, and the individual believer in whom the Spirit dwells—which facilitates "resonance."

## True Revivals Illustrate Resonance

When we see "resonance" in in our consulting, we realize we are witnessing something the Church has seen throughout its history. The stories of the great revivals contain many episodes of the Spirit "sweeping" through an audience in response to the preaching of an evangelist, both to convict and convert a large number.

But the Spirit does not just produce conversion. Like the revival of Ezra's and Nehemiah's time (Nehemiah 8-9), the Spirit swept through that Jewish audience convicting them of their sin, and producing weeping, grief, and repentance. The mark of spiritual resonance is that it occurs across an audience/congregation *simultaneously*. It is neither mindless nor can it be manipulated, as is sometimes seen in the ministries of modern spiritual hucksters.

Whether during the ministries of George Whitfield, Jonathan Edwards, and John Wesley during the First Great Awakening in the English colonies or the ministry of Jonathan Goforth, Presbyterian missionary to China, examples of and witnesses to such corporate, simultaneous resonance with the Spirit abound, both in converting the lost and convicting the saved. Here is one example from Jonathan Edward's ministry:

> ". . . the Spirit of God began extraordinarily to set in and wonderfully to work amongst us . . . Presently . . . a great and earnest concern about the great things of religion and the eternal world, became *universal* in all

---

[12] Torrey, 93.

parts of the town and among persons of all degrees and of all ages. The noise amongst the *dry bones* waxed louder and louder . . . And the work of conversion was carried on in a most *astonishing* manner and increased more and more. Souls did, as it were, come by flocks to Jesus Christ" (Emphasis his).[13]

John Wesley describes a similar experience in his Journal: "at times the whole multitude in a flood of tears, all as it were crying out at once."[14]

None of this should surprise us. A mystical union binds all members together in the body of Christ. When Divine communication occurs thorough the Holy Spirit, every spiritual gift/part will resonate with His Voice. Love (as 1 Corinthians 13 describes) enables us to hear God's heart over the Divine tension between the gifts. Often God's feelings get imparted as well, breaking the hearts or releasing the joy of those present.[15]

This "hearing His Voice" signals that the body is now "in tune" or "in sync" with the Divine Head, and that all the parts of the body know and feel it. The Scriptures will confirm this communication, *never, ever* contradict it. The Holy Spirit communicates God's attributes to and through His gifted children, and the gifted members bring the entire body in line with the Divine Head.

---

[13] Jonathan Edwards, *A Narrative of Surprising Conversions.* (Banner of Truth, London) 1965. P.30

[14] John Wesley, *Journal,* Vol 2, pp. 230-231, quoted in Arnold Dallimore, *George Whitefield: The Life and Times of the Great Evangelist of the 18th Century Revival* (Banner of Truth, London), 2001, Vol 1, p. 324.

[15] To learn more about how God speaks to churches corporately in times of revival see *The Path of Revival: Restoring Our Nation One Church at a Time* by Mark Barnard (ChurchSmart 2009).

It is a beautiful, elegant dance of love between the Bride and her Husband. It makes the local church unique in the world...and *very* attractive to a watching world.

# Chapter 4 Discussion Questions:

1. What are some dangers of only hearing from a few of the spiritual gifts in your ministry?

2. As you reflect on your staff and or leadership team, what spiritual gifts are under or overrepresented?

3. In your own words, how would you describe "spiritual resonance" among the gifts.

4. If a local church has Jesus as its Head, how can ministry leaders stay in touch with Him?

5. Is your church safe enough for all the gifts to operate? If not, what needs to be healed to facilitate this?

6. If Jesus was your dance partner, how well would you say you are following His lead (as an individual and as a church)?

# Chapter 5

# Resonance Among the Gifts in Acts

Making decisions in line with God's will for a ministry is always a challenge. The process is usually messy because most leadership teams contain a high degree of diversity. There is tension between differing cultures, experiences, education, age, and ultimately spiritual gifts. How does a group of culturally diverse, multi-gifted, and uniquely shaped leaders discern the Lord's leading together?

We (Mark and Ken) are Biblicists. We believe unequivocally and without apology in the authority, power, and centrality of the Scriptures to a believer's faith and life. If it is not taught in the Scriptures, we do not buy it! Therefore, it was important for us to see the principles we have defined worked out in the Bible, and not by proof-text either.

In addition to Revelation 2-3 where the Spirit speaks with clarity to seven local churches, there are three accounts from the book of Acts that demonstrate resonance in action. The first relates to the need for direction in ministry outreach. The second reveals how resonance (and dissonance) work when sorting through a thorny theological/doctrinal issue. The last addresses how to discern between several compelling ministry choices.

These three accounts cover the kinds of decisions church leaders regularly face. We know that one must be careful drawing their doctrine from Acts because of its transitionary nature between the age of Law and of Grace. Many things were changing as the Church moved away from Judaism and the Jerusalem temple. But Acts also demonstrates how the apostles and the Church learned to dance this new dance in which the Lord was leading them, and that's what we need to understand.

## Resonance in Ministry Direction in Antioch

Saul (Paul) and Barnabas had returned to Antioch after delivering a much-needed gift to the Jerusalem church (Acts 11:29-30; 12:25). From the account of what follows, we discover several principles which can guide leaders who seek direction or confirmation from the Spirit for their ministry:

> *Now there were at Antioch, in the church that was there, prophets and teachers: Barnabas, and Simeon who was called Niger, and Lucius of Cyrene, and Manaen who had been brought up with Herod the tetrarch, and Saul. While they were ministering to the Lord and fasting, the Holy Spirit said, "Set apart for Me Barnabas and Saul for the work to which I have called them." Then, when they had fasted and prayed and laid their hands on them, they sent them away* (Acts 13:1-3).

Several things should strike us here. The ministry assignment Saul and Barnabas received came directly from the Lord *speaking to a group!* This occurs when they are corporately focused on drawing near to God to pray and listen. It is also very different than the Lone Ranger approach we generally take when it comes to ministry calling and assignment. These men represent the *plurality* of leaders in Antioch.

Luke lets us know some of the differences between these men. They had a variety of spiritual gifts, teaching and prophesy getting special mention. Additionally, we know that Barnabas had the gift of encouragement, and Saul/Paul possessed that of apostleship and evangelism. Differing spiritual gifts tend to pull leaders in different directions, but here we see all these strong gifts used in a desire to know the Spirit's leading.

They also had very different backgrounds, some of which could create tensions among them. Saul, the former Pharisee from the Roman colony of Tarsus, had viciously persecuted the church. He prayed near Manaen, who was raised in aristocratic circles with the hated Herod the Tetrarch. Barnabas was a Levite (named Joseph) from Cyprus. Simeon, called "Niger" (which means "black"), could have been a black African. Some believe Lucius was also black since he was from Cyrene in North Africa. That does not even include the conflicting Jewish and Gentile cultures, which we know characterized the Antiochian congregation. Diversity on top of diversity, a sure recipe for tension and messiness in discerning a direction for ministry!

Such was the diversity of gifts, ethnicities, and backgrounds that shaped the leadership team at Antioch. Kent Hughes refers to them as "amazingly heterogeneous . . . a racially integrated group of go-getters."[16] Yet their differences reveal how Jesus intends churches to discern His leading by the Spirit.

Another key in hearing from the Lord is avoid distractions. Verse 2 gives us their focus: *"While they were ministering to the Lord . . ."* The Holy Spirit spoke and made His will clear while they focused on worshipping and interceding to Jesus as a group. The word "ministering" (Gk: *leitourgeo*) is the basis for our word "liturgy" and is used for serving the populace as a public servant or a priest. The Spirit's message did not arrive following a brief word of prayer before this board meeting! It came while they focused on ministry

---

[16] Ken Hughes, *Acts: The Church Afire* (Wheaton: Crossways, 1996) 174.

to the Lord and not on themselves. These leaders learned that's when God spoke to them. When was the last time your board meetings saw "ministry to the Lord" as an agenda item?

Fasting intensified their focus: *"While they were ministering . . . and fasting."* Fasting in this case involved food, for preparing and eating food was a distraction. But a broader definition helps us understand fasting today: giving up something we feel we need in order to gain something we cannot live *without*. Fasting is self-denial of a need in order to focus and concentrate our hearts and minds in prayer. Discerning the voice of God demands our *full* attention, and food, TV, smart phones, social media, and other things we think we need get set aside while we seek it.

After a time of fasting, prayer, and ministry to the Lord, this diverse group of leaders heard *collectively* the Holy Spirit speak.

> *"While they were fasting and praying, the Holy Spirit said "Set apart Saul and Barnabas . . . Then, when they had fasted and prayed and laid their hands on them, they sent them away."*

While these leaders ministered to the Lord, He ministered right back to them. They received this *corporate* direction; the quiet voice of the Holy Spirit spoke to them all! Their focused and undistracted hearts gave them "ears to hear" Him clearly.

Interestingly, we are not told *how* the Holy Spirit spoke, but it is likely He communicated His will the way He does today—through the spiritual gift of some of the leaders present. Once spoken though, the statement *resonated* with everyone present, and they together took responsibility to lay *their* hands upon Saul/Paul and Barnabas. Once the will of the Lord became clear, they responded immediately, sending these two popular leaders of the Antiochian church on their first missionary journey, and what a journey it would be! The world would not be the same as a result.

It is worthwhile to assimilate this pattern into your modern leadership context. If you have not learned or experienced how God uses the diversity of gifts, personalities, cultural backgrounds, and ethnicities to communicate to His body, He is more than willing to teach you. But Acts has more illustrations of how this process works.

## Resonance at the Jerusalem Council

As we said earlier, there is natural tension between spiritual gifts because they represent Divine attributes that are in tension in God's heart (such as justice and mercy), a tension into which He invites us. But believing leaders often see such tension as *opposition or conflict*. They fear it, avoid it, and worse, often squelch that which is natural to the nature of the gifts. Silencing gifts in tension is like severing a tendon in the body. You make the body much *weaker*.

We fail to recognize that it is the *same* Holy Spirit speaking through these *gifts in tension*. Since He speaks through diverse, dissonant gifts, we recognize His will when "dissonance" becomes "resonance." When believers truly seek the will of God and the guidance of the Spirit of God, they need to work in tension until God gives them that spiritual resonance.

Love is the oil that keeps the tension from becoming frictional and destructive. Unloving attitudes, actions, and words are red flags that tell leaders a deeper issue exists, one like Jesus speaks to the Ephesian church about in Revelation 2. Maintaining love and respect in the midst of the passionate differences our spiritual gifts express will lead us to resonance.

Acts 15 gives us a beautiful picture of this "tension process" of spiritual gifts at work during the Council of Jerusalem. The early Church struggled with the transitionary nature of what was happening when it came to Law and Grace. Talk about tension!

Some of these pharisaical individuals followed Paul and Barnabas from city to city, "correcting" their teaching. Acts 15:1 tells us, *"Some men came down from Judea and began teaching the brethren, 'Unless you are circumcised according to the custom of Moses, you cannot be saved.'"* This is about as significant as a doctrinal issue gets, touching the very heart of the Gospel. Is there some additional "work" that we must perform to gain salvation?

What then unfolds shows us that even the most difficult theological issues can be resolved when we listen to all the spiritual gifts God provides and respond with humility. This doctrinal dispute caused a strong "debate and dissension" in Antioch with Paul and Barnabas. Unable to come to a unified understanding that resonated with everyone in the Antioch church, the "church" wisely *"determined that Paul and Barnabas and some others of them should go up to Jerusalem to the apostles and elders concerning this issue"* (15:2). They decided as a body that they needed outside input, people who had more collective wisdom and experience. The Jerusalem church provided that.

Once in Jerusalem, the apostles and elders gathered, but it was also *more* than just them. Everyone wanted to hear the report of what was happening among the Gentiles:

> *When they arrived at Jerusalem, they were received by the church and the apostles and the elders, and they reported all that God had done with them. But some of the sect of the Pharisees who had believed stood up, saying, "It is necessary to circumcise them and to direct them to observe the Law of Moses"* (15:4-5).

Jerusalem immediately entered the debate. There was already a "sect" of people voting on the outcome. Here is where you watch the power of collective resonance when facing a thorny issue: *The apostles and the elders came together to look into this matter* (15:6).

Luke gives highlights of the debate and discussion. Peter starts the conversation (as usual, given his gift of leadership), and gives an impassioned argument of how God spoke to him in a dream about not making distinctions between Jews and Gentiles (15:7-11). Given who he was, we know he carried clout, but the passionate exercise of his gift doesn't resolve the dissonance or division in this case. *"All the people kept silent"* (15:12), which is often a sign resonance has not been reached.

This is key to understanding how God uses the different members of the body. The bigwigs do not always have (or get) the answer, and that is a "God-thing." God intends that the process build up the body, and the higher the tension in the process, the stronger the body will become, just as any strength coach will tell you. They knew to wait for resonance in the Jerusalem church, and Peter's fiery input did not create it.

Paul and Barnabas spoke next and added their gifts and experience to the mix (15:12), but that does not produce resonance either. Three apostles with powerful gifts, speaking with passion about the subject, even as the believing Pharisees had done earlier. In the modern church, this would be the basis for a raucous, ugly split and a new denomination forming. We know it's true!

But into the midst of a critical theological debate, where the conclusions and exhortations of recognized leaders fail to "win the argument," how does resonance work? A non-apostle with the gift of wisdom does what we have witnessed happen numerous times in churches wrestling with painful issues. James is an interesting character. He was the half-brother of Jesus, known as "the elder." Tradition tells us he became the "pastor" of the Jerusalem church.

Luke tells us that James waits until they finished. This is the nature of the gift of wisdom. It seldom interrupts but waits until there is silence. James then affirms the input from Peter and paraphrases Amos 9:11-12 to give a biblical context for what he will suggest:

> *After they had stopped speaking, James answered, saying, "Brethren, listen to me. Simeon has related how God first concerned Himself about taking from among the Gentiles a people for His name. With this the words of the Prophets agree, just as it is written,*
>
> > *'AFTER THESE THINGS I will return,*
> > *AND I WILL REBUILD THE TABERNACLE OF DAVID WHICH HAS FALLEN,*
> > *AND I WILL REBUILD ITS RUINS,*
> > *AND I WILL RESTORE IT,*
> > *SO THAT THE REST OF MANKIND MAY SEEK THE LORD,*
> > *AND ALL THE GENTILES WHO ARE CALLED BY MY NAME,'*
> > *SAYS THE LORD, WHO MAKES THESE THINGS KNOWN FROM LONG AGO.* (15:13-18)

He then offers a practical solution:

> *Therefore it is my judgment that we do not trouble those who are turning to God from among the Gentiles, but that we write to them that they abstain from things contaminated by idols and from fornication and from what is strangled and from blood* (15:19-20).

Spiritual gifts never violate or contradict the Word of God. Even seeking God's answer in a tough, conflicted situation will also never drive a wedge between the Spirit and the Word. We need to develop our discernment when it comes to recognizing the Spirit's voice through the mouth of a gifted individual, learning to be prayerful and submitted to the Spirit in our own lives.

After James speaks, what happens next is a thing of beauty and a great model for how we should handle similar situations.

Luke records three evidences of that resonance:

1. *"Then it seemed good to the apostles and the elders **with the whole church** . . ."* (15:22)
2. *"It seemed good to us, **having become of one mind** . . ."* (15:25)
3. *"For it seemed good **to the Holy Spirit and to us** . . ."* (15:28 – Emphasis ours)

The sharpness of the conflict melts, and the dissonance changes to resonance within the body of the Jerusalem church. Spiritual resonance results in this kind of *clarity*: a unified sense of direction, not just with leaders but with the "whole church," and a sensible plan (*"it seemed good"*) to implement what the Holy Spirit was saying to them. The early church thus avoids a crisis that easily could have derailed unity and produced a major split!

Failing to understand the "principle of resonance" operating here has resulted in the splits that now characterize the Church. Most leaders have probably "tasted" resonance at some time, but do not know how God made it work. When we consult with churches in pain, we often see that the leaders don't know how to listen to what the Spirit is saying to them through their body's gifted people because no one has ever taught them how.

1 Corinthians 12 describes how every body part is valuable and needed for the church to function in a healthy way, but leaders lean on their own understanding or the works of secular leadership gurus instead. They don't know how "every body part" could work in decision-making and/or conflict. Paul illustrates this to the Corinthians earlier when he rebukes them for going to secular law courts to resolve conflicts against each other:

> *Does any one of you, when he has a case against his neighbor, dare to go to law before the unrighteous and not before the saints? **Or do you not know that the saints will judge the world? If the world is***

*judged by you, are you not competent to constitute the smallest law courts? Do you not know that we will judge angels? How much more matters of this life? So if you have law courts dealing with matters of this life, do you appoint them as judges who are of no account in the church? I say this to your shame. Is it so, that there is not among you one wise man who will be able to decide between his brethren, but brother goes to law with brother, and that before unbelievers?* (1 Cor. 6:1-6 Emphasis ours)

God gives all His churches the spiritual equipment (in the form of their spiritual gifts) to do this kind of tough work. Using our gifts like this trains all of us for future roles as judges, both of the world and of angels!

Unfortunately, just like the Corinthians, modern spiritual leaders misunderstand and misinterpret the tension the gifts naturally produce as God invites His children into His heart. They then wonder why their "body" reels or resists their leadership in response. It is because the congregation does not *resonate spiritually* with their decisions.

## Forbidden by the Holy Spirit

After presenting this material on resonance at a church conference, a former engineer familiar with acoustics took me (Mark) aside to explain more accurately the way resonance works. "*Every* material object has a particular frequency," he said. "If an object gets bombarded with a frequency that is the same as the object's frequency, that object begins to vibrate. It 'resonates' with the external frequency applied to it." This is seen most commonly in tuning forks. If you vibrate a tuning fork and place it next to another tuning fork of the same frequency, *both* forks will begin to vibrate.

However, he went on to explain that resonance is usually a *bad* thing. Resonance starts with vibration, but if ignored, the vibration can turn into *oscillation*. This oscillation, or "wobble," can cause serious damage, like an opera singer shattering a wine glass with her voice or an airplane engine that flies apart due to the effects of "flutter" (a term used to describe resonance gone awry).

The Holy Spirit energizes the gifts He gives us individually and those gifts "vibrate" to life within us, signaling that we are on His "frequency." The Holy Spirit indwells every member in Christ's body while at the same time remaining distinct from them.[17] When we respond to Him, we *enjoy* it because we sense that we are in tune with Him and were *made* for this. However, sometimes the Spirit prompts us to use our gift and we ignore or resist this prompting. This causes inner dissonance and discomfort. We are now "out of sync," and we term this discomfort a "lack of peace" (1 Cor. 14:33). Resist over a length of time and the prompting of the Spirit gets "quenched." We stop sensing His prompting because we have changed frequencies.

What happens at the individual level also occurs at the group level in ministry. In Acts 16:6-10 Paul and his companions were delivering the decree from the Jerusalem Council among the Gentile churches as well as looking for new opportunities to preach the Gospel. They followed the Holy Spirit as He led them through Asia Minor and had learned to listen to Him carefully and together to sense His leading. What is intriguing about this passage is how the Holy Spirit *stopped* them, prevented them from doing something, a curious set of experiences that are instructive for leaders.

> *They passed through the Phrygian and Galatian region, having been forbidden by the Holy Spirit to speak the word in Asia; and after they came to Mysia,*

---

[17] Donald Macleod, *The Person of Christ* (Downers Grove, IL: IVP, 1998)141.

*they were trying to go into Bithynia, and the Spirit of Jesus did not permit them; and passing by Mysia, they came down to Troas. A vision appeared to Paul in the night: a man of Macedonia was standing and appealing to him, and saying, "Come over to Macedonia and help us." When he had seen the vision, immediately we sought to go into Macedonia, concluding that God had called us to preach the gospel to them.*

God put a hold on their plans to preach in Asia Minor. The opportunity would come later in a big way (Acts 19 where "the Word" spreads from their ministry in Ephesus to all Asia), but at this juncture God had other plans. Here is where leaders have to ask themselves, "Are we following God's plan or our own?" When leaders together seek resonance, they must give the Spirit the right to *stop* them as well as move them. What appeared like an obvious ministry opportunity to Paul's team was not on God's agenda, at least not yet.

What is *not* clear is this: how did the Holy Spirit *communicate* the restriction? We are not told details, but it was undeniable in their *collective* minds. They listened to what each was sensing. The Spirit operated in them all to hinder or disquiet them, prevent them from expending time and energy resources in something He did not choose *at that moment.* They felt the unified resonance and submitted to the Lord's prohibition.

Moreover, it happened twice. *"They were trying to go into Bithynia, and the Spirit of Jesus did not permit them."* The Holy Spirt again said "No, don't!" and they all heard Him. Most believers are familiar with the individual experience of this, primarily by means of "closed-door circumstances": a cancelled flight, a flat tire, an illness, etc. that prevents us going somewhere that, it is later discovered, would have been disastrous. Paul's mission team sensed that *the Spirit of Jesus* put up a roadblock to them.

## Paul's Night Vision and God's Call

It left them with an obvious question though: "Lord, where *are* you leading us?" They did not have to wait long. Paul fell asleep in Troas and received a compelling vision in a dream. It was not the result of strategic planning or a demographic study. Paul's night vision, known as "The Macedonian Call," prompted ministry in an unanticipated direction and opened the door for the Gospel into Europe.

The whole group reflects on the meaning of the dream and decides this is what God is calling them to do. Luke, who is now part of this group, tells us this by using the 1st person plural: *"When he had seen the vision, immediately we sought to go into Macedonia, **concluding** that God had called us to preach the gospel to them"* (Emphasis ours). As the Jerusalem Council showed, apostolic input is not beyond the discerning and confirming voices of other spiritually gifted leaders. The dream and vision of one person is not sufficient to discern God's will for a group (Col. 2:18-19). We need the right interpretation of the vision; others who can confirm that it is of God and means what we think it means. The Apostle Paul was not above this. You should suspect anyone who says they are.

*Sumbibazontes*, the Greek word for "concluding" means "to knit together." A.T. Robertson, writes, "This word here gives a good illustration of the proper use of the reason in connection with revelation, to decide whether it is a revelation from God, to find out what it means for us, and to see that we obey the revelation when understood."[18] D.A. Carson writes, "They *collectively* concluded

---

[18] A.T. Roberson 248.

that it [Paul's vision] meant they should press on for Macedonia"[19] (Emphasis his).

This collective operation involved Paul sharing his dream with Silas, Timothy and Luke, and then all four men processed and prayed about the dream's content and together sensed the Spirit leading, "*calling*" them to Macedonia. They now knew why He had closed the previous doors. Don't be impatient when gifted leaders in your group have hesitations about your ministry's direction. With love and respect undergirding your relationships, be willing to hear what the Spirit is saying through each other's gifts and come to a unified sense, a "resonance," about what He wants.

I (Mark) know of a church that went on a forty-year "wander through the wilderness" like Israel after Kadesh-Barnea. Facing a decision about a building program, people with the gift of discernment expressed misgivings and the leadership alienated and silenced them. That's the dangerous side of ignoring, devaluing, or suppressing the gifts God gives the body. It can misshape your ministry for *decades*, long after the original decision is passed. We have witnessed it repeatedly in the conflicted churches with which we consult. Operating with the input of one or just a few gifts when facing a major decision or a moral crisis quickly frays the fabric of congregational trust. People feel they are not heard or that their input doesn't matter. It also ignores why God gave the ministry those gifted people at such a time.

But there is always balance. Spiritual gifts like discernment may have to submit to one with the gift of teaching, wisdom, or leadership on occasion. It all depends on resonance. In God's economy, no one person gets all the answers. All the gifts function in mutual submission and accountability, and sometimes as Paul

---

[19] Carson, 164.

says, the "unseemly" gifts, or less significant people (like the 9th grade girl of the earlier illustration) become more important for discerning what the Spirit is saying, especially if there is pride or elevated self-importance in a ministry. The Spirit helps each person sense how their gift (with its unique perspective) helps reveal God's heart and will in each situation.

Here's the bottom line: A leader who thinks that he/she alone hears from the Holy Spirit and is unwilling to submit their "leading" to input from the other gifted people in the ministry, is very likely going to pull a "king Saul." They will do spiritual damage to themselves and break trust with others. They may have the business savvy or charisma to pull off what appears to be "successful," but the impact will be short term, and, ultimately, they leave a broken skeleton (and a lot of wounded people) in the body behind them.

We can take another thing from the account of the "Macedonian Call." Paul and his companions doubtless struggled through the restrictions God placed in front of them as they travelled, wondering why doors to valid ministry were shut. But they had resonance, so they together knew they were where they were supposed to be, even if they didn't understand why (yet). Faith, by necessity, would play a key part.

We live in a day of strategic visions where everything gets laid out in one, five, and ten-year plans. People with the gifts of administration are strong on planning; those with a gift of faith, not so much. A "night vision" leading a pastor in an unexpected direction could throw a church's staff into a tizzy, uncertain whether it was God or the jalapeno poppers he had for dinner that gave him such vivid dreams. Gifts of administration and wisdom would speak up (if permitted) in that staff meeting and the gifts of faith and encouragement probably also (We flesh this out in the last chapter.).

## Other Characteristics of the Process

We don't want to be so locked into our routines that God can't break in to move or adjust us. On the other hand, we don't want instability and uncertainly to characterize our leadership. God is not a God of chaos but of peace. Paul's experience with his companions in Troas teaches us the importance of trusting the gifts around us to provide the resonance we need in sensing God's voice and will. It also prevents many of the destructive conflicts we see all-too-commonly in churches.

God brought clarity to Paul and his companions; it made sense to *all* of them on the team and they were unified in the course of action they should take. They hadn't known why God closed the previous doors, but they trusted their unified sense of what the Spirit was saying and obeyed. His leading them through Asia Minor taught them to listen to each other as they each listened to Him. He prepared them for the moment when the new door opened.

The same methodology sustained them when things got difficult down the road in places like Philippi and Athens. God did things that confirmed they were on the right path, opening the hearts of people to the gospel and sending earthquakes if need be. If you learn to listen to all the gifts God gives your leadership team and flock, there will be stories and signs of God's validation that you are truly following His plan.

Sometimes on leadership teams someone *not* in charge becomes adamant that their viewpoint is the right one. Those *in charge* must know the Spirit works this way. The adamant one may be right, or, if nothing else, needs to be heard. At such moments, the Voice of the Spirit speaks quietly but firmly. Being attuned to each other's gifts and loving each other becomes crucial. Our gifts make us passionate about what we sense and feel. When articulating a minority viewpoint, love and respect must reign and recognize all gifts need to be heard. Don't get tricked into "being right" at the expense of love. We are doing our job in the body when we give the input our gift impresses on us, but we become cancerous to the body if we become divisive and/or lose our love. Unfortunately, this happens all the time.

Without love, gifted church leaders begin to sound like a "noisy gong or clanging cymbal" (1 Cor. 13:1). That's the perfect example of *dissonance* between spiritual gifts rather than God's intended harmony. Love turns the dissonance to resonance. It also helps us accept the tension between the gifts as normal, and "endures all things" until that resonance is achieved.

If resonance on an issue is elusive, *wait* on the Lord, *seek* Him. This is also a part of God's training regimen. Remember, these experiences manifest the partnership we share with Him. He has you and your team in His gymnasium and, like the best Coach, He is working you out to make your body stronger. The stronger you become, the more useful you become and the more responsibility He can entrust to you. Thus the partnership with Him becomes profound and powerful.

Resonance confirms that you have heard from Him. Wait for it. The *process* of learning to listen to God through what the Spirit says through all the gifts He has provided is as important as any decision you could make. Don't assume you know the Lord's timing. You don't. Paul (and others) eventually made it to Asia and Bithynia, but God knew the timing was not right in Acts 16. He had something else He wanted them to accomplish first. It is His right as Lord to do that.

Finally, understand that resonance as we have described it is about the confirmation of a positive decision. United *agitation* is also a form of resonance that you are about to do the wrong thing. Don't ignore this! United "disquiet" is probably the way Paul's team recognized they were not to go into Bithynia. A wise leader will empower all team members to say, "I don't feel good about this."

Don't rush to a decision without resonance or *collective confirmation* and make certain you don't suppress the voices of those who might feel disquiet. Resonance requires each team, board or staff member to yield his or her perspective, laying it down at Jesus' feet before resonance occurs. We can't expect the Lord to reveal His agenda with clarity while we refuse to release our agenda.

Moving forward without resonance between the gifts ends up doing more harm than good. It breaks trust and receives Divine discipline. When spiritual leaders won't listen to the Holy Spirit speaking through the gifts God allotted to their ministry, out of love He reproves and disciplines them (Rev. 3:19). They experience corporate pain. If they continue to ignore what the Spirit is saying, He *amplifies* the intensity of His discipline and the body feels more pain. If they still will not listen, they will start to lose valuable things: attendance, resources, missional traction, unity, and love.[20]

We will return to some of these examples later and examine them for further principles. The key here though is learning how to listen to the "body," with all its God-given spiritual resources. It is not optional equipment for a modern spiritual leader. Better to wait until you learn how to have spiritual resonance with your team than to move forward without it.

---

[20] To learn more about how God disciplines churches see *Healing the Heart of Your Church* by Ken Quick (Amazon 2018).

# Chapter 5 Discussion Questions:

1.  How does Acts 13:1-3 demonstrate that we need the gifts of others to determine God's will?

2.  How does Acts 15 (Jerusalem Council) model how difficult theological questions can be resolved?

3.  Has God ever stopped you from taking certain actions that you later realized would have been disastrous? Example?

4. What does the existence of dissonance between the gifts tell us?

5. How willing are you to release your ideas, plans and will to better discern how God is leading your ministry?

6. Is your ministry currently experiencing corporate pain because of past leadership decisions that lacked resonance?

# Chapter 6

# Testing the Messages that Come through Spiritual Gifts

In our ministry to churches, we regularly witness the breath-taking power of the Lord Jesus Christ to speak to, heal, and restore a ministry that has experienced devastating wounds, splits, abuse, broken trust, and/or moral defilement. We had to put these things through the sieve of the Word of God to "prove" what was of the Spirit and what was not. We owe this kind of careful examination to ourselves, to the constituencies we serve, and to the larger body of Christ.

From this process we learned paradigm-shifting principles. For instance, corporate healing (or guidance) requires that the ministries gathered for such a purpose use their gifts and learn how to hear from Christ *as a body*. This was not based on American political philosophies about democracy, but on solid biblical principles and models. But these were things we were never taught in seminary or in church. The Scriptures helped us, providing teaching, reproof, correction, and training in righteousness as we wrestled with the meaning of resonance at the corporate level.

Because of the inherent dangers of people *thinking* they are hearing from God when they might not be, we handled such things with utmost care. As we served more and more congregations in pain, we documented the patterns, the "ways" in which the Spirit worked at that corporate level that were unique and transcended the lines of denomination, ethnicity, church structure, and church size. And He also built in protections, "checks and balances," if we know to use them.

## The "ABCs" of Proving All Things

We want to return to Acts and nail down some of these "checks and balances," providing application for you and your leadership team. By comparing some of the collective meetings in Acts, a biblical model emerges for testing the validity of the corporate messages your ministry receives through its spiritual gifts. Leaders are responsible for developing the wisdom, insight and discernment to recognize spiritual resonance, what is from God and what isn't.

We term this "the ABCs of proving all things," a mnemonic for different occasions in Acts where a collective body of believers, both small group and large council, sought and discerned the will of the Lord. "A" stands for the leaders of Antioch (Acts 13:1-4). "B" is for the people of Berea (Acts 17:10-15). "C" is the Council of Jerusalem (Acts 15:1-30).

The specificity, scope and nature of the message changes with each setting. In Antioch immediate action is called for and Paul and Barnabas get sent on their first missionary journey. At Berea, their effort to examine the Scriptures confirmed the message they heard as from God, and they responded to it. This, Luke tells us, was "noble" on their part. The Council of Jerusalem led to a critical "policy decision" that resulted in a letter from the "mother church" to all the Gentile converts/churches, and it impacted the Church positively for centuries to come.

The means through which the group discovered the Lord's will varied in each case. In Antioch, they were *"ministering to the Lord and fasting"* (Acts 13:2). In Berea, *"they were examining the scriptures daily, to see whether these things were so"* (Acts 17:11). And at the Council of Jerusalem, *"the apostles and elders came together to look into this matter"* (Acts 15:6). God's will is discerned differently in each context but all produced resonance and led to significant spiritual effects.

## Antioch as a Model

At Antioch, as the leaders were fasting and praying, *"the Holy Spirit said . . ."* (13:2). He may have spoken to their minds simultaneously, but it is far more likely that this message came through one of the gifted individuals present (Luke tells us there were those with the gift of prophesy in the group.) and, after a time of further prayer and fasting, there was resonance. God's used this to communicate a *calling* on the lives of two key men in the congregation.

Timothy received a similar summons related to his gifts and calling, something about which Paul reminds him in both epistles bearing his name:

> *"Do not neglect the spiritual gift within you, which was bestowed on you through prophetic utterance with the laying on of hands by the presbytery"* (1 Tim. 4:14).
> *"For this reason I remind you to kindle afresh the gift of God which is in you through the laying on of my hands"* (2 Tim. 1:6).

Those elders who commissioned Timothy told him something prophetically about his calling (connected to his spiritual gift) as they laid hands on him. It is likewise clear from Paul's exhortation that Timothy could "neglect" this calling and his gifts, demonstrating that "the spirit of the prophet (or whatever Timothy's gift) is subject to the prophet (Timothy)."

The Antioch model provides direction in uncharted waters, when we are unsure what God wants us to do. We see this illustrated in the previously discussed Acts 16:6-7 when the Holy Spirit forbade Paul and his companions' entry into Asia and Bithynia. As Paul determined to go to Jerusalem (Acts 20:22-23), the Spirit also communicated to him what awaited him through a few gifted individuals (21:4, 11, 14). Paul evaluates these messages and, while the warning resonates with him, the conclusion of his friends (that he should not go to Jerusalem) creates *dissonance* in his spirit. He knows what the Lord wants him to do, even if his friends covet his safety. Sometimes prophets get the message straight but not the application! They don't know everything.

But this model is not the only way God communicates and there are some dangers to it. The weakness is that it leans on a *subjective* experience. You wonder if you heard the Spirit or if you are experiencing "wishful thinking." Therefore, the examples we see in Acts are all *collective*. The other members of the body confirm the subjective message. The body thus protects us. In Antioch, the elders didn't settle for quick assent. After they heard from the Lord they prayed and fasted some more. They gained resonance about what the Spirit said, and their "laying on of hands" of Paul and Barnabas testifies to their collective confirmation.

Paul writes *"Do not despise prophetic utterances. But examine everything carefully; hold fast to what is good"* (1 Thess. 5:20-21). John writes, *"Beloved, do not believe every spirit, but test the spirits to see whether they are from God, because many false prophets have gone out into the world"* (1 Jn. 4:1). The Biblical emphasis is on examination and discernment of anyone who says they have a message from God.

We know false prophets and false apostles exist, and Jesus commends the church that puts them to the test (Rev. 2:2). Such testing requires *collective* resonance, not individual. Subjective leadings are vulnerable to our all-too-human personalities, experiences, motivations, interpretations, wishes, and prejudices. At Antioch, confirmation came through the resonance of a group of gifted and experienced church leaders who loved and cared for each other.

## Berea as a Model

At Berea they confirmed the witness of the Holy Spirit through the study of God's Word. The Bereans were *"examining the Scriptures daily"* (Acts 17:11) to determine if the Apostle Paul's message was biblical. Notice the collective nature of it too. All these activities are "body" exercises. This methodology has resonated with Christians through the ages. The *confirmation* of the Scripture is a key component in the validation of any message coming through a spiritual gift. It should *always* be a part of collective leadership discernment—everyone using their gifts in love—to study to show whether a message/teaching is "approved."

The strength of the Berean model of "proving" a message rests on the authority of God's Word. They *"received the word with great eagerness,"* (17:11) but not with so much eagerness that they didn't fact-check Paul. The Bereans model what John writes about in 1 Jn. 4:1, "testing the "spirits." Paul was the new preacher in town. He came with a unique/new message of their Messiah dying and being resurrected, one that both excited them and raised concerns. They asked themselves, "Is what we are hearing true? Does it line up with the Scriptures?" They used the Word of God as their only rule of faith and practice. Paul's testimony, even as a former Pharisee, was not enough.

In the same way, when any gifted individual shares what they believe God is saying about an issue our ministry faces, no matter *who* it is (famous author/teacher, pastor, elder, key giver, etc.) or what their role is, we must be careful. This is where the modern Church could learn from the early Church. How do we discern if what we are hearing is true, especially if it is "new?" We must do what the Bereans model for us: *collectively* discern if the message in harmony with the teaching of Scripture.

This is a sure, though not a rapid, safeguard. Draw upon those in your body that have gifts which confirm or warn you about what you are hearing and listen carefully. But then collectively study the Word of God to "see if these things are so."

The weakness of the Berean model is that sometimes our collective understanding of the Bible is vulnerable to our denominational heritage and history, motivations, misinterpretations, and cultural distortions. Don't trust your own gift in isolation from others. We are afflicted by many prejudices which affect how we see things as individuals. When we find ourselves struggling to "rightly divide the Word of truth," consider gathering a Council of godly wisdom as modeled by the Jerusalem church in Acts.

## The Jerusalem Council as a Model

In Acts 15, as the Jerusalem church gathered to discern what the Spirit was saying about Gentiles needing to become Jews (through circumcision) to be saved, elements of both "A" (Divine communication through spiritual gifts) and "B" (Divine communication through the Scripture) operated. The spiritual gifts of Peter, Paul, Barnabas, and James are at work as they speak, but James also quotes Scripture as validation of what he sensed the Spirit saying. Their "council" approach—trained and experienced leaders using their gifts *and* the Scripture—brought *clarity*. Their process allowed all the gifts to operate, and God granted "resonance" when they reached His conclusion.

The result was the peaceful unsnarling a very difficult and divisive doctrinal challenge. The history of Protestantism is the *exact opposite* since the Reformation. We have split, split, split, split, and when we were done with that, we split some more! We, who proudly believe we have the truth, have shown ourselves incapable of staying unified. We ought to be so ashamed!

When James shared what he felt God was saying to him, it *"seemed good to apostles and elders with the whole church"* (15:22). We don't know how many Jerusalem believers that entailed but it was likely a group of several hundred if not a thousand people, and we know that the believers from the Pharisees, who had been most adamant about circumcision being necessary for the Gentiles, were present too (15:5).

This peaceful resolution and revolutionary conclusion motivated the Church of the early centuries to use "Church Councils" to resolve many of the problems they faced (and the Church's great creeds come from some of them). But there is no "magic" in just holding a Council, and having one guarantees nothing. It is rather love operating in the use of spiritual gifts and understanding the Scripture, then waiting for corporate resonance that made the Jerusalem Council "work."

The strength of this model of discernment is that it can deal with large, potentially divisive doctrinal issues. It combines the spiritual gifts of experienced leaders, the testimony of Scripture, and a knowledge of how God worked in the past. But it is probably not the model to use when seeking guidance in a specific situation, like Paul experienced in Acts 13 or Acts 16.

The model of Council of Jerusalem represents a process that facilitates peacefully dealing with major disputes in the body of Christ. Not that there won't be tension—that is *absolutely* normal given the nature of the gifts!—but if the body has learned how to wait for resonance, for the Spirit to make them of one mind, they can resolve the toughest and most divisive of issues. It may also, on a localized level, represent what the Apostle Paul recommends for the Corinthians as the alternative to going to secular law courts (1 Cor. 5). It could help a board discern a balanced new policy for your church, or a denomination decide on doctrinal dispute that will impact all its churches.

# Chapter 6 Discussion Questions:

1. What do the letters in the "ABC's" of proving all things stand for?

2. What do you think will happen if you move ahead with a ministry decision while lacking the resonance modeled in Acts 13:1-3 or Acts 15?

3. How do the Bereans model testing those who claim to have a new message from God for your ministry?

4. How does seeking resonance among all the gifts keep us from idolizing certain individuals in our ministry?

5. Which spiritual gifts might be the first to raise a concern about a new teaching? How much freedom do those gifts have to operate in our ministry?

6. How does humility relate to proving the messages that come through spiritual gifts?

# Chapter 7

# Spiritual Gifts and Maturity

In a perfect church, every believing member lovingly exercises their spiritual gifts aided and empowered by the Holy Spirit all the time. In a perfect church, staff and lay leaders earn the trust of those they lead by learning to listen to *all* the gifts in the body while modeling *agape* love in the midst of the tensions those gifts create. In a perfect church, leaders work through differences by seeking spiritual resonance, and are patient to wait on the Lord for it. All this manifests the way the Bride of Christ lovingly relates to her Husband, pleasing Him by her faith, and awaits His will to be revealed. He then delights to show up in her midst every time she gathers in His Name.

Unfortunately, as someone observed of *actual* church life:
> *To dwell above*
> *with saints we love,*
> *that will be grace and glory.*
> *To dwell below*
> *with saints we know,*
> *well, that's another story!*

God's beloved and gifted human instruments are flawed and broken. Instead of what's inside a perfect church, visualize your leadership team (along with you) sitting around the boardroom table with all their emotional baggage, wounds, selfish ambitions, unsavory motives, distractions, dysfunction, *and* spiritual gifts. It is probably not hard to visualize because that's your reality. How do you deal with such personal shortcomings that regularly sabotage the effort to achieve resonance?

The answer is growth and maturity. Look carefully again at the apostle Paul's words to the Ephesians, often the foundational verses of many a "philosophy of ministry":

> And He gave some as apostles, and some as prophets, and some as evangelists, and some as pastors and teachers, for the equipping of the saints for the work of service, to the building up of the body of Christ; until we all attain to the unity of the faith, and of the knowledge of the Son of God, to a mature man, to the measure of the stature which belongs to the fullness of Christ.
>
> As a result, we are no longer to be children, tossed here and there by waves and carried about by every wind of doctrine, by the trickery of men, by craftiness in deceitful scheming; but speaking the truth in love, we are to grow up in all aspects into Him who is the head, even Christ, from whom the whole body, being fitted and held together by what every joint supplies, according to the proper working of each individual part, causes the growth of the body for the building up of itself in love. (Eph. 4:11-16)

Paul describes the perfect church! But he also describes the process that leaders, their roles, and their gifts are to take to get there.

## Using Resonance to Move to Maturity

The key to spiritual growth in Ephesians 4, both individual and corporate growth, is that *each and every body part functions "properly."* This enables the body to "fit together" and "hold together." This must be the goal of spiritual leadership, to equip the saints to grow in this way, to properly function with their gifts. The way we get off track, according to the Apostle, is through a catalogue of human-based philosophies and machinations: "winds of doctrines," "trickery of men," "craftiness and deceitful scheming." We witness boards and staffs leaning on secular methodologies far too often to achieve spiritual ends (as if the thing could be done).

Again, when Paul says, *"the spirits of prophets are subject to prophets"* (1 Cor. 14:32), in context he means that the speaker with a speaking gift (in this case, prophesy) decides how, when, and how long to exercise their gift. Preachers do this all the time by having their preaching/teaching gift "time-bounded" in a service. Paul uses prophecy, the most passionate of the gifts (in our experience), to illustrate the principle of "the greatest example standing for all lesser ones." This principle of "the gift being subject to the gifted one" applies to *every* spiritual gift, not just prophecy. We *choose* whether our gift operates or not.

We see this in several New Testament examples. Paul regulates his gift of apostleship. He says to the Corinthians: *"What do you desire? Shall I come to you with a rod, or with love and a spirit of gentleness?"* (1 Cor. 4:21) He has a choice how to exercise apostolic authority. Timothy had the gift of evangelism and Paul exhorts him, saying: *"Do not neglect the spiritual gift within you, which was bestowed on you through prophetic utterance with the laying on of hands by the presbytery"* (1 Tim.4:14). Timothy could either use or neglect his spiritual gift.

A ministry leader can likewise hinder or neglect the expression of his or her gift. If a board or staff discuss a moral failure of someone in their constituency, the Spirit will prompt the strong expression of several gifts, particularly the prophetic gift which reveals God's attribute of justice, and the gift of mercy revealing that Divine attribute to the group for balance. But if one of those "voices" holds back because they feel inferior or worse, if they are silenced because they are perceived to be "judgmental, ungracious" (the prophetic gift is often seen this way) or "weak on sin" (the mercy gift often is viewed this way), then the body gets weakened (1 Cor. 12:15).

## Dynamics which Derail Resonance

One way we derail resonance is by failing to consider what God may be saying/doing when tensions between gifts run high. One of the most gut-wrenching scenes in the book of Acts is the conflict between Barnabas and Paul over whether to take John Mark with them on their second missionary journey. Luke records the sad conclusion: *"Their disagreement was so sharp that they separated"* (Acts 15:39).

What makes their conflict even more painful is that it comes on the heels of the beautiful unity resulting from the Jerusalem Council (Acts 15:1-29)! How could godly leaders sense and follow the Lord's leading in the first half of Acts 15 and end the same chapter in a dispute that divided a close-knit team? As godly as they were, Paul and Barnabas made a mistake we see spiritual leaders at all levels make *all the time*. They mistook *dissonance* between their gifts for *dissension and irreconcilable division*.

Barnabas, with strong gifts of encouragement wanted to invest in Mark, just as he had invested in Paul. Complicating matters further, Mark and Barnabas were family (Col. 4:10). Mark's history with the early church goes back to the house owned by his mother, the sight of a prayer meeting that saw Peter miraculously released from prison (Acts 12).

But, in Paul's eyes, Mark was a quitter. He had deserted them when things got tough on their first missionary journey. Paul's apostolic calling, evangelistic gift and the scars on his back made him less tolerant of quitters. Paul's gifts were in strong tension with Barnabas' ministry of encouragement.

In this case, they allowed dissonance between their gifts to become divisive. In the process, they lost sight of what God wanted to do in their midst. He used the dispute over Mark as a pry bar to redirect both Paul and Barnabas' ministries. Each had a calling to fulfill, one investing in kingdom workers and the other in expanding the kingdom. God used the division to reach both Cyprus *and* Europe.

Paul went with Silas and continued to see God work through his ministry. We see the same blessing on Barnabas' ministry to Mark. Mark goes on to become a confidant of Peter. Peter calls him his "son" (1 Peter 5:13). He and Paul reconcile at some unrecorded point in time (Col. 4:10). Mark takes up with Paul in his travels (Philemon 24). To cap it all off, in Paul's last recorded letter he declares Mark's usefulness to him (2 Tim. 4:11). Barnabas' faith in Mark was rewarded. Then, in addition to all this, Mark graces all of us through the Gospel bearing his name!

So the next sharp dispute you have with a fellow believer, take time to discern what God may be saying, doing, or trying to accomplish through the dissonance between you (this works in marriage too). Try to see if spiritual gifts are at work, giving you both differing perspectives. If sharp (and severe) enough, take time to fast and pray for discernment. Then God will grant you the ability to discern between dissonance between your gifts (and what He may be saying through it) vs. dissension because of self-will.

Character flaws *can* undermine our spiritual gifts. John Mark's cowardice and unwillingness to endure the hardships of Paul and Barnabas' first missionary journey caused him to bail on them, his spiritual gifts unused for a time. Fortunately, the Bible leaves room for growth in our character. Years later, when Paul calls for John Mark to join him, he had clearly grown and proven himself (2 Tim. 4:11).

## A Safeguard for Unhealthy Expressions

In some cases (probably more than we care to admit), an insecure leader may insist that his/her perspective matters the most, because, in their insecurity, he or she *needs* it to matter most. An oversized self-estimation that shuts down the other gifts reminds us of Paul's question, *"If the whole body were an eye, where would the sense of hearing be?"* (1 Cor. 12:17) The body has been given the gifts because God still knows "it is not good" for us to be alone. In such cases, you end up with a dysfunctional body, broken trust, weakness, and no resonance. God intended that there be no islands, no "one-person show" in ministry.

A previously mentioned biblical precaution helps limit such unhealthy expressions of the gifts, but it requires courage and love to implement. Paul again says, *"Let two or three prophets speak and **let the others pass judgment"** (1 Cor. 14:39, Emphasis ours). We can debate what the gift of prophecy is, but no matter your definition, whether you view it as "forth telling" or "foretelling," the Bible says it is *not beyond scrutiny*, no matter who is doing the prophesying.

Paul exhorts the Corinthians to hold prophets accountable, to scrutinize what they say, and *look for resonance*. Does the body hear the Spirit in what the prophet says? Prophets are accountable for the content of their communication, and Paul implies that they are not always right. Everyone who possesses this gift must submit what they say to the judgment of the body. It is a part of developing healthy leadership. Woe to the individual who attempts to manipulate or coerce this! Carson cautions:

"a prophet who treated his or her prophesy as so immediate and direct and untarnished a product of divine inspiration that it should be questioned by no true believer, would not only be stepping outside the Pauline restrictions but would, presumably, ultimately fall under the suspicions of the church."[21]

Paul addresses prophets in *"Let the others pass judgment"* but it implies that *all* those exercising their gifts should be willing to submit the expressions of their gift to other gifted souls for confirmation or correction. This requires humility, love, and trust, but that is good! Most churches experience a failure of nerve at this point, unwilling to lovingly correct a pastor or key influencer, and the body quickly gets out of whack as a result.

Such correction teaches us to "tune into the Spirit" more effectively. We become more adept at using our gifts, more sensitive to the way the Spirit speaks. One can still exercise his/her gift without feedback/input/loving guidance by others in the body, but if an issue requires resonance within the body, then we need mutual accountability. We should never elevate any gift (or gifted person) to the place where they can say, *"I have no need of you"* to the other gifts.

## Reality?

To get your leadership to exercise their gifts in a healthy way, you must disciple them (or each other) to the place where they each become non-anxious about the future of the ministry (Prov. 3:5-6). We ought not to lean on our own understanding about this. Insecure and immature behaviors dissipate as leaders learn to trust in the Lord and His enablement.

---

[21] Carson, 121.

Visualize your staff and/or ministry leaders sitting around the boardroom table, or in a congregational business meeting. Instead of anxiety over certain conflict or resistance or distrust, you experience happy comradery, enjoying the unity of the Spirit, people exercising their spiritual gifts in mature wisdom, committed to and loving each other, and always achieving resonance in what the Lord of your ministry is saying to you.

This is not a dream. We are witnesses to the fact that there is *nothing*, no subject or issue so difficult or painful that the body can't discern what the Spirit is saying if they use their gifts this way. It requires a reorientation of leadership priorities to help your leaders get free from what threatens the healthy expression of their gifts, and to attune themselves to the Voice of the Spirit.

However, one key lesson we have learned at Blessing Point is, if your church has a history of painful crises, you need to address the unhealed wounds in your corporate history before you can hope to see your leaders get healthy. Pain in the body of your ministry is always a sign of something being wrong. If, when you assess the history of your ministry and you discover the pain is cyclic, then you are experiencing Divine discipline for something unrectified.[22] God won't let you off the hook until you discern what the issue is, and resonance is the key to doing this.

---

[22] To learn more about how God disciplines churches see *Body Aches: Experiencing and Responding to God's Discipline of Your Church* by Ken Quick (ChurchSmart 2009).

# Chapter 7 Discussion Questions:

1. According to Ephesians 4:11-16 what is the purpose of spiritual gifts?

2. In Ephesians 4:16, how does love set the tone for the way differing gifts are to work together?

3. What does the ability to self-regulate one's spiritual gift suggest about our need to be sensitive to the Holy Spirt in the expression of our gift?

4. When might the ability to self-regulate one's spiritual gift lead to passivity in the use of our gift?

5. What might happen if the rest of the body does not hold an insecure/immature member accountable for his/her oversized self-estimation?

6. What are some ways you can help your church leaders become non-anxious about the future (Prov. 3:5-6)?

# Chapter 8

# Failing to Discern the Body (and Its Gifts) Rightly

Much has been written on how God speaks to us as individuals, but the bookshelves are bare when it comes to helping leaders know how God speaks to and guides a ministry. Yet the biblical emphasis, whether through all the epistles of the NT or the Seven Letters of Revelation 2-3, is on that *corporate* communication.

We have come to believe He speaks to churches *constantly*. We hear him when we have our "ears" attuned to what *"the Spirit says* (present tense in the original) *to the churches."* (Rev. 2:7, 11, 17, etc.) The Spirit speaks through the spiritual gifts He providentially places within in our ministry constituency. But sometimes "speaking" to a church does not get through, because they are not listening! Jesus sometimes communicates through painful *discipline* and sometimes He must *knock* loudly (Rev. 3:19, 20)!

The Corinthian church's behavior, like the Laodicean, required that Jesus turn up the pressure. It required a STOP order! How did Jesus get His point across to these churches? It comes out most clearly in 1 Cor. 10 and 11. In Chapter 10, Paul describes the disciplines God inflicted upon the Israelites in the wilderness when they misbehaved, warning the Corinthians that "These things were written for our instruction," and repeating the phrase "Let us not _____ like they did...", then describing some kind of painful corporate discipline.

Their specific corporate misbehavior (at least the one Paul focuses on here) comes toward the end of Chapter 11 around the Lord's Supper: *"For in your eating each one takes his own supper first and one is hungry and another drunk"* (11:21). The church came together to share in a "love feast" and at the end came a celebration of the Lord's Supper. Those who arrived early scarfed up the food and drink like a bacchanalia, getting drunk and leaving crumbs for late arrivers.

They shattered the all-important symbolism of the Lord's Supper, causing Paul to issue a dire warning. He explains the symbolic nature of the bread and cup with words recited at most Communions today. They took Communion in an "unworthy manner" and the consequences come because they make light of its symbolic significance: *"For he who eats and drinks, eats and drinks judgment to himself if he does not judge the body rightly."*

Whoa. That final phrase should stop us in our tracks. What does it mean to "judge the body rightly" around the Lord's Supper? Does it mean building a "fence" around Communion, excluding unbelievers or non-members of our denomination from participation? Does it refer to limiting communion to adults who have professed Christ?

Rather, the significance of the Communion is two-fold. First, we are to remember the price Jesus paid to bring each believer to salvation and into union with Him. But, second, He didn't save us to be lone rangers. His body and blood were given to unite us *collectively* into His "body" as His Bride. We are not His Bride as an individual believer, but only as a collective body, called the Church. We are individually members of that larger body.

We share in His flesh and blood and Spirit, and it makes us unique in the world. It is the nature of the "marriage" of each local church and its members to Jesus. Paul describes this in marriage terms in Ephesians 5:

> *for no one ever hated his own flesh, but nourishes and cherishes it, just as Christ also does the church, because we are members of His body. FOR THIS REASON A MAN SHALL LEAVE HIS FATHER AND MOTHER AND SHALL BE JOINED TO HIS WIFE, AND THE TWO SHALL BECOME ONE FLESH. This mystery is great; but I am speaking with reference to Christ and the church* (Eph. 5:29-32).

Notice it is not Christ and the believer, but Christ and the *church* that Paul describes. That is the "body" we must discern and judge rightly, a body we entered through the giving of what the Communion elements symbolize.

*"Failing to judge the body rightly"* then, means taking Communion when members of that body behave in ways that wound, disrespect, or sin against others in the body. What an offense it must be to Christ when members of a church body go on month after month, year after year, taking communion when their "body" is filled with distrust, division and strife.

Everyone in the body is responsible for what is happening in Christ's eyes if you are a part of that body. Being intimately linked like this also means we cannot wound, disrespect, or do any other kind of damage to another believer without injuring ourselves. The "one flesh" union is that deep. Do we think so little of what Christ gave His body and blood to do to unite us? We insult Christ and He *feels* it as insult!

The behavior of the Corinthians in Chapter 11 led to *Divine discipline* (11:29-32). Paul states in 11:30, *"For this reason many among you are weak and sick and a number sleep."* Church prayer lists *normally* are dominated by folk who need physical healing.

Church prayer meetings *normally* are consumed with concerns for those who are sick. Perhaps this ought not to be "normal."

Many North American churches are also weak, sickly and a number sleep. "Sleep" is Paul's euphemism for death, used in 1 Corinthians 15:51 where he says, *"We shall not all sleep."* God disciplines a body by "graduating" some of its members, and ultimately churches themselves, to the sleep of death.

## Implications of Failing to Judge the Body Rightly

Several implications arise from the Corinthians' failure here. First, the Lord was completely aware of what they were doing. The way they took communion injured His body, the equivalent perhaps of a slap in Jesus' face. But it wasn't all. Paul had already upbraided them for their divisions over favorite teachers, going to court, failure to discipline immorality, marital relationships, their use of their Christian freedom, spiritual gifts, and gender roles.

The Lord was not willing to overlook that which offends Him in their body. Every time modern church leaders ignore known problems in the body, they affront Jesus in the same way. Neither does He overlook it in our churches.

Second, Jesus actively communicates with churches by *disciplining* them. Discipline *is* communication! He does this out of love when their behavior does damage to His body and His purpose for it (Rev. 3:19). This is *corporate* Divine discipline, which is different from individual discipline. The pain of it impacts the whole church, but particularly leadership. It is the equivalent of the way God dealt with Israel nationally. It happened to them as an example to us.

Jesus told the members of the well-heeled Laodicean church that they were wretched, miserable, poor, blind and naked, not to mention lukewarm and nauseating spiritually. Those traits would have struck a chord with a community known for its wealth, eye salve, clothing industry and tepid, sulphur-flavored water.

Third, it is no accident that Paul's teaching on spiritual gifts follows his teaching on the spiritual danger they were in. The gifted people God has given the ministry can help restore what they are losing if every gift is valued, even the "less-seemly" ones, and they learn to exercise them in love. If you ignore, neglect, or abuse these gifted ones, your body grows weaker. Every joint and ligament helps the body grow. If we fail to listen to all the gifted members, Jesus uses corporate Divine discipline—many weak, sickly, and dying, painful divisions, distrust, etc.—to get His point across.

Because of the nature of our ministry at Blessing Point, we hear and see modern examples of this principle. A prominent lay leader dies unexpectedly in a church where the board is given to ruling with an iron fist. A pastor has a heart attack while preaching on Christmas Eve in a church where his spouse wounds and abuses church women. A group of rebellious church elders see one pass away, another has a heart attack, and a third experiences a devastating family crisis in a short period. In one divided congregation, the pastor takes his own life with a gun in the church foyer. Another church suffers a history of leaders—pastoral and lay—who become mentally ill while serving. We know the churches where these have happened and more.

Happenstance? The work of the Devil? Shall we believe in God, but think all these traumas escape His notice? If they don't, do they have a message for us beyond "That's life in the sin-cursed world?"

An epidemic of sickness may or may not speak to sin in the lives of those who are ill. As it did in the Corinthian church, it may speak to something going on in your church that offends the Lord. For the

Corinthians it had to do with taking communion (a beautiful symbol of unity) while actively divided. God is *not* mocked!

Based on the number of weak and sickly ministries in North America, Jesus is shouting to us today just as He did to the Corinthian church. We often snicker at the immaturity evident in their congregation. We may look down on the Corinthian church while blind to what Jesus is saying to us.

If you suspect that your church's problems are rooted in the unhealthy ways your body's "parts" have historically related to each other (as was the case at Corinth), would you be willing to suspend communion until you address your church's corporate problems?

We know that such a move would take courage and perhaps offend congregants. It might cost you your job as pastor, or as a lay leader. And certainly, no such decision should be taken without gaining resonance among the rest of your leaders and Jesus. This is the challenge of church leadership that resonates. We may not like what we hear through the interplay of spiritual gifts or what it will cost us to align ourselves with Jesus's design for our ministry. But what do you think will happen if, having heard from the Lord through the interplay of spiritual gifts, you ignore His Divine communication?

# Chapter 8 Discussion Questions:

1. How does ignoring the input of some members (and their gifts) relate to "failing to judge the body rightly"?

2. If Jesus speaks through spiritual gifts to a church and leaders ignore that input, who are they really ignoring?

3. How do you explain that a loving God would discipline His churches?

4. Those who fell "asleep" in the Corinthian church became symbols of a deeper problem. What was the deeper problem?

5. If Jesus knew what was going on in the Corinthian church and sought to address it (because the leaders had not), how might that occur in modern churches?

6. Have you ever been guilty of snickering at the condition of the Corinthian church? If so, how might this blind you to the true condition of your own ministry?

# Chapter 9

# A Case Study in Gifts and Resonance

As a way of sharpening the reader's discernment, we thought we'd end with a case study. This story is a combination of dynamics that Mark and Ken have witnessed at work in numerous churches and denominational conferences. Sometimes we are a part of such things but do not fully understand what we are witnessing or the principles behind them. We believe that a narrative like this will aid in dissecting the process within one's own ministry.

## The Staff Meeting

Lead Pastor Griffin Patterson bounded confidently into the morning staff meeting. He could barely contain himself as he paced the spacious but outdated boardroom. Like the church he served, the boardroom reeked of status quo. At one end of the room stood a small library of dusty commentaries. At the other end was a projection screen. A dozen black leather chairs framed a long weathered mahogany conference table. In spite of the environment "Griff," as he was known by his staff, could not remember the last time he felt this giddy to begin a staff meeting at Fairway Church.

Next to arrive was the always punctual Administrative Pastor, Tom Himtha. Tom slipped into the room, laptop under his arm, taking his predictable seat nearest the wall socket. He plugged in his first-generation MacBook Air into the outlet. A former manager for an accounting firm, Tom was new to ministry and known as a notorious penny pincher. This explained his dinosaur of a laptop. He couldn't justify the expense of a new one when his old one still worked, slow as it was, and absent of any battery power.

Zack Rogan, the youth pastor, Seth Dealer, the children's ministry coordinator, both entered the room at the same time. Seth laughed as he took his seat no doubt still reacting to one of Zach's daily morning jokes. The rest of them would soon hear it, too, if Seth did not beat him to it. Yesterday they had been discussing staffing needs within their respective ministries and both had looked a little flummoxed when Griff debriefed them about it. He was pleased to see them relaxed today. Zack's ministry had seen an uptick in conversions of late and he had recruited some of Seth's lay leaders to meet the need for discipleship with the new converts. As a result, Seth found himself stretched thin, his corral of children's ministry workers dwindling.

He may have been the last to arrive, but Pastor Rob Roberts was the most colorful of the bunch. Fueled by a combination of high-octane energy drinks and an outgoing personality, the church's visitation pastor never entered a room without everyone noticing. The rest greeted him as he neared his seat. Zach leaned far across the wide table and gave Pastor Roberts a high five.

"Okay, People," Griff got things started with his usual greeting. "Rob, before you sit down, could you close the door please?"

"My pleasure!" Rob boomed, his voice echoing against the walls of the conference room. The door shut with a gentle thud. Rob plopped down in one of the chairs and took a swig of his latest caffeinated concoction.

Griff continued, a smile spreading across his face. "Guys, I am *super* excited about today's staff meeting. I have an idea for a new ministry, one that has real potential to increase Fairway's reach. But before we get into that, Seth, would you open us up in prayer?"

"Sure, but after can I tell you guys a joke?" Griff's eyes told him no. He lowered his head and said, "Let's pray!"

"Lord, we thank You for the opportunity to serve you here at Fairway. We confess we don't have all the answers for this ministry. We need Your wisdom. Please be our Teacher and Guide today. Help us to honor You in all we do. Amen." The others echoed Seth's "amen."

Griff, unaware that his feet were tapping rapidly wasted no time getting started. "Guys," he began, "I believe the Lord gave me a vision for a new ministry that would be a perfect fit for Fairway and our community. It might sound a little crazy at first, but hear me out. You know we are smack dab in the middle of a planned community. We have 30,000 residents and 12,000 golf carts which people use to get from one end of town to another. There are 100 miles of paved paths throughout the city."

Griff was pleased to see all his staff leaning in taking in every word.

"What if we tapped into the local culture and began a drive-in service for golf carts? It would be an outdoor venue and would create a whole new vibe for worship. With a name like Fairway Church it would make perfect sense. We have three golf courses in town and several others nearby. I've seen a church in a Florida retirement community doing the same thing and I think we could pull it off here. We could call it a 'Green Church Service.' It would be 'green' because no one would use any gas to get to it. Most golf carts are electric."

"Hey, that's a good one, Griff," Zach piped up. The word 'green' could also ties into the local golf culture."

Griff nodded at Zach and continued. "Exactly, Zach. The piece of land that's for sale across from the church would be a perfect location. I've done some preliminary research and talked to the landowner. We can purchase it for $500,000 and I know the whole project will only cost about a million dollars. All we need is a Jumbotron which we could mount on our building across the street. It would be like a modern-day tent service without the tent!"

Whether it was the caffeine or his personality, one could never quite tell the difference with Pastor Rob. "Hey, I *like* that!" He said this while clapping his knee with his one free hand.

"Great idea, Griff," he said. "Worshiping on the lot across the street from the church would be like holding a service in the middle of nature. How cool would that be? Since we would be meeting outside, people could bring camp chairs, kids could be free to wiggle and we could even bring something to drink to the service."

Seth interrupted Rob's machine gun delivery and said, laughing, "Something to drink to the service? Rob, you're *never* without something to drink!"

Rob laughed in return and said with a sarcastic tone, "Ha ha. Well, I may favor liquid refreshment, but, really, the possibilities for an outdoor service *are* endless. I bet there are planned communities all across the United States. We could come up with a whole new ministry model. Jumbotron churches in fields across America." Rob, free now of his drink opened his arms out as wide as possible. "We could change the face of church worship, the whole getting back to nature theme is in vogue. Didn't John the Baptist preach out in the open, Jesus too? Even John Wesley preached outside. Plus, our older folk who don't drive cars anymore could come on their golf carts. This could be just the kind of thing to reach aging baby boomers. They're out for adventure and this would be a novel way to satisfy their itch." Pounding the table Rob bellowed, "I'm all in guys!"

Griff noticed that Zach's eyes also reflected strong enthusiasm. No longer able to hold it in, Zach blurted out, "Think about the possibilities for evangelism! Lots of people would come to the service out of curiosity. We could set up a small stage in front of the screen and on nice days preach outside. If the weather gets bad, we can invite them inside. I can imagine a whole new pool of people to reach with the gospel!"

Griff quickly noticed that Tom, the church administrator, appeared tense. He was. "Guys," he said, his voice terse, "I am afraid that the elders are going to think we've been sleeping in staff meeting again."

"Huh, why is that?" Griff probed.

"Because," Tom replied, "You're all DREAMING. Have you seen our inflows lately? Revenues are down. Where do you think we'd get a million dollars, if that's really all this project costs?" Rob's tension was beginning to take over the enthusiasm in the room. "I know that for the audio to work, you would have to buy an FM transmitter, not to mention the Jumbotron and related equipment. The electrician would cost a fortune." Tom leaned in toward Griff, and then scanned the others seated around the table. "Have *any* of you looked at the last financial statement?"

Rob spoke first hoping to turn the tide of this conversation. It had gone so well, until Tom poked the preverbal balloon risking the air of this plan to disappear completely. "Come on Tom! Financial statement? God owns the cattle on a thousand hills. Certainly, He would sell a few to help us pay for this world changing ministry venture!"

As it turned out, Tom wouldn't let it go. His voice was controlled, but strong. "Have you walked that parcel of land? That lot has been vacant for a reason. No one has bought it because no one wants it. Not only is it over priced, it sits in a flood plain."

Rob piped up, "You can't let a little water stop you!" I bet that can easily be filled in."

Sensing a break in the exchange, Seth hoped to bring some levity and reason to the growing tension. "The Bible has a lot to say about "claiming the land." I could develop some curriculum around that theme and we could tie it into the vision for this project." We could schedule the teaching in all departments and Griff could preach on it too."

Griff, getting more firm as he was sometimes prone to do, said, "Look guys." His voice grew passionate. "We need to move on this. We are only on this planet for so long. We have to get something done for the kingdom. We have to fulfill our mission as quickly as possible. Who cares what obstacles we might face?"

Appearing to reflect on his earlier comment Seth quietly countered, "But Griff, do you think the timing is right? Because I'm not so sure. I have this whole series on Revelation that I've been developing with the Christian Education committee. I'd hate to see that get derailed. Our people need this teaching so they can be equipped to live the Christian life under increasing pressure from the world."

Zack was getting irritated now. Though they worked together, his interests often clashed with Seth's. "What's more important, Seth?

Leading people to the Lord through a new outdoor venue or *another* teaching series? Don't we have enough teaching already?"

Seth felt a little hurt by Zack's dig. "Dude, it's obvious. If you don't *teach* believers a biblical worldview, how will they do apologetics?"

"Yeah," Zack shot back, "But, if you never lead anyone to the Lord, who will there be to teach?"

Rob, getting bored with what seemed like a spiritual version of the chicken and the egg conundrum, tried to reframe the subject. "Okay guys. We've been on this carousel before. I think God is big enough to accomplish both things at the same time if we just take a step of *faith*."

"I am all for trusting God," Tom replied. "Who isn't? But we have to make sure we are doing things in the *right* way."

Griff looked troubled. Sometimes he had to admit that Tom reminded him of his overly strict father. He tended to react to Tom the same way he did with his dad. He would passively submit to his overly powerful father, but fume on the inside. "Tom," Griff said, "You're starting to discourage me. I really wanted to put in an offer on that land next week."

Tom, looking directly at Griff knew his words would sting. "I don't think that's very realistic, brother."

Before Griff could react, Seth offered a compromise. "Maybe we need to pray about it some more."

Griff really didn't hear Seth. He was lost in buried emotions when he responded. "It just seems like a no brainer. Seth, you're not getting hung up on the details too are you?"

"No." Seth replied, "I just like to think things through, that's all."

In his most matter of fact, authoritative, business-like voice Tom stated, "I have some major concerns about this idea. It seems way too risky given our current financial landscape."

Griff winced as Tom's next statement cut deep into that part that reminded him again of his father. "You would be irresponsible to pursue this 'vision' at this time."

Griff took a deep breath. "Okay guys, I think that's enough for today. I think it might help if you took Seth's advice and prayed about this. I will do the same. Right now we don't have enough unity around the idea to proceed. Next week is General Assembly in Nashville. Let's bring this issue up again after we get back. Perhaps the Lord will give us some clarity by then."

Griff brought the meeting to a close with the following prayer. "Lord, I want to reiterate what Seth said in his opening prayer. We need your wisdom. In Jesus' name. Amen."

## The General Assembly

*Knock! Knock! Knock!* The moderator, Rev. Thomas Micks, briskly slammed his gavel on the podium to open Tuesday afternoon's business session at General Assembly in Nashville.

Reverend Micks stood erect, the model of perfect posture. He was the kind of man who made a bow tie look good. His white hair and full beard gave him the look of a distinguished Santa Claus. With his reading glasses perched halfway down his nose, he looked out on the sea of faces including those from Fairway Church. He announced, "The committee on theological issues will now present the revised statement on abstinence from alcohol among licensed workers. Will the chairman of the committee please approach the microphone and share the revised statement with this body?"

"Mr. Moderator, the current policy requiring licensed workers to take an abstinence pledge would be replaced by the following statement:

> The Bible teaches moderation in the use of alcohol. Therefore, grace should be shown to licensed workers who choose to drink alcohol. Grace should also be extended to licensed workers who, for conscience sake, choose not to drink alcohol.

Respectfully submitted, The Committee on Theological Issues."

"Thank you, Mr. Chairman," the moderator replied.

Reverend Micks paused to clear his throat. Some noticed a twitch in one eye and thought they could see fear in the other. The auditorium was eerily silent. For the change in policy they were voting on represented a shift that was a hundred years in the making. Many older ministers in the room were against the change. Younger ministers were for it. As moderator, the great burden that rested on Reverend Micks was to hold a potentially divisive discussion in a God honoring fashion. The vote to approve or disapprove the measure would immediately follow.

Reverend Micks began, "Before we open the meeting for discussion of the revised statement allowing licensed workers to partake of alcohol in moderation, I would like to ask for a personal privilege. I am confident you will assent to my request once you learn of it. Because of the special sensitivity of this issue and because it marks a potential shift in a long standing policy and because it affects every minister in our denomination, would you be kind enough to gather in groups of two or three and ask the Lord to help us as we address this issue? After a few moments, I will close our time in prayer."

A sea of 5000 faces nodded in assent. Everyone knew that this was the right thing to do. People leaned across chairs or shifted in their seats to face each other. A cacophony of prayers ascended from the crowd. From the platform, Reverend Micks could not make out the words. He could only hear the humming of many in prayer. Their collective tone ebbed and flowed like a field of wheat in a gentle breeze.

After a few minutes, Reverend Micks closed his eyes and silently prayed to know how to pray. He then stammered out the following, heavy with emotion. "Heavenly Father, we have before us an issue of great concern to many. We want, no, we *need* Your mind on this matter. Additionally, Lord, we need the grace to discuss this matter without wounding the body of which we are all a part. Many groups have divided over like issues and we don't desire to be among them. You prayed for our unity in John 17 and we covet that unity now. We know there are strong feelings on both sides of this issue. Would You enable us to reach a conclusion on this matter that honors You and maintains our love for one another? To the glory of our Lord and Savior, Jesus Christ. Amen."

Four microphones were strategically positioned around the auditorium. Reverend Micks opened discussion, "The matter is before you. Is there any discussion? Yes, the chair recognizes microphone number two."

"Mr. Moderator, Thank you for your opening prayer." The middle-aged delegate with thinning hair paused. He clutched a prepared statement in his trembling hands. "It set the tone with which I want to speak *against* the proposed change to our policy of abstaining from alcohol among licensed workers. We know that for one hundred years our denomination sought to model abstinence from alcohol and our ministers took a pledge to do so. I don't need to review the benefits of this policy or the scriptural basis for it. Those who have gone before us found ample reason in Scripture to ask us to make such a vow. All of us here have participated in that vow. One of the difficulties we face in changing the policy is that of identifying the party to whom we made the vow. If it was merely to an organization, then the possibility of changing course is a viable one. However if we took the vow of abstinence *as unto the Lord*, a greater assembly than this may one day call us to account should we break such a vow." Does God take vows seriously? I believe ample biblical evidence exists to show that He does. This concerns me. If the pledge was made to God, does voting to change the policy release those who have already taken a pledge?

As the man stepped back from the microphone, Reverend Micks replied, "Thank you for your comments. The chair recognizes microphone number four."

At the microphone stood a younger delegate, one that looked like he could have been the son of the first speaker. "Mr. Moderator, I would speak in *favor* of the change in policy. When the original policy was first written our fledgling movement was in the midst of a reaction against another larger denomination. That group had become extremely progressive. They commingled with the world, engaging in theological and social compromises. We were birthed with a predisposition to interpret Scripture in a way that guarded against theological error and ungodly, worldly behavior."

"Now, by speaking in favor of the change in policy, I do not mean to say that I am in favor of ungodly behavior." The man gathered his thoughts distracted by the soft laughter that spread from his comment. Committed to press through he continued, "I simply mean to say that the policy was birthed out of a reactionary mindset. Over

115

the years our movement has suffered because of our lack of engagement with the world in areas where inroads could have been made without compromising our faith. We have often been accused of legalism. We have not participated in the arts. We promoted the stigma of attending movies, dancing, and Sunday activities. Truly, there is value in abstaining from some of these things, but I would suggest we have drawn the line along that which the Pharisees did, several steps back from the danger itself."

"Some say that a change in policy regarding drinking alcohol is a compromise with culture. I would argue that such a change allows us to be better salt and light in culture. Instead of being against culture, we want to engage culture with the hopes of influencing people for Christ. Changing the policy would lessen the stigma we have placed on the use of alcohol. It would make lost people feel more comfortable with us and lead to opportunities to share the gospel. Finally, if I may be so bold, I would call on us to repent of our long history of legalism about such matters."

With the delegate's final words, a murmur of apparent agreement spread across the audience.

"Thank you for those comments." Reverend Micks understood the importance of staying calm. All eyes were on him. "The delegate at microphone number one. You have the floor."

"Mr. Moderator, I would speak *against* changing the policy in question." Several in the room applauded lightly. "It is true, as the last speaker pointed out, that the original stance of our forefathers was framed in a different setting than the one we face today. However, I would guard against labeling those who went before us as *legalists*. These were men, like us, with strengths and weaknesses. They looked at the world around them and acted to protect the reputations of ministers within our movement, not to mention the reputation of the movement itself. I do not and would not fault their decision. We would have likely constructed the original policy in the same way had we been in their shoes."

"What looks like legalism in the rearview mirror of our history resembled godly wisdom to the men who wrote the original policy. Even if they did act out of legalism, let us not be so harsh in judging them that we overlook the possibility of our acting with license now."

"As we were praying together a few moments ago, a verse of Scripture came to mind. May I share it with you as it relates to the historical aspect of the current policy?"

Rev. Micks nodded.

"Thank you. It's in Proverbs 22:28 and it reads, "Do not move an ancient boundary stone set up by your ancestors."

"All of us have submitted to the current policy. I don't believe it needs to change. If the world thinks us strange because we abstain from alcohol, let them think what they like."

"The chair thanks the speaker from microphone number one. The chair acknowledges your concern about moving an ancient boundary stone set up by our ancestors. However, the rules committee has informed me that if such a change were to be made, this would be the proper setting in which it could be changed legally without incurring the Lord's displeasure. The original policy was adopted by this body, such as that body was, one hundred years ago. The body gathered today has the constituted authority to change the policy. We meet for such a purpose. Had the national office made the change in policy without consulting this body, the wisdom of such a move would be questionable at best. Discussion to this point has already revealed strong feelings on both sides of the matter. If headquarters had handed down a new policy without allowing the body to be heard on the issue, it would have wounded the body and likely compromised the body's trust in its leadership. All that to say, should this body decide to change the current policy, the rules committee informs me we could do so without fear of acting improperly."

The room was silent.

Reverend Micks continued. "The chair recognizes microphone number three."

A rough looking, middle age man grabbed the mic with shaking hands. "Mr. Moderator, I would *plead* with this body not to change the current policy. We live in a day when alcohol and recreational drug use is as common as breathing. Many of us in ministry today came to Christ out of a background tainted by such activities. Many more will come to Christ out of a similar background in the days to come. For those of us predisposed toward addictions, because of our past, a change in policy removes a safeguard that has kept us from falling back into old habits. My family history is pock-marked by alcohol's effects; mental illness, broken relationships, and poverty. I am also a recovering alcoholic. Thank God I've been sober for over 25 years."

The room broke into applause.

The man raised his left hand in acknowledgment but also because he had more to say. "I do not speak against the measure out of legalism nor out of avoiding compromise with culture but out of the pain that arises from behaviors the current policy prohibits. Even though I now abstain from alcohol, my children are still vulnerable to the leftover unhealthy behaviors associated with me and my family of origin. I pray, nearly every day, that my kids will grow up to be less dysfunctional than me."

"A moment ago, we mentioned moving an ancient boundary stone. The Bible talks about several kinds of stones, the millstone and the cornerstone, for example. The one I am thinking of now is the stumbling stone. To change this policy would cause many in our midst to stumble in their consciences. And what will most of us gain by changing the policy? Ministers would be free to drink a glass of wine with dinner or share a beer at a Barbecue. I doubt the benefits would outweigh the temptations this change in policy would create."

Reverend Micks thanked the speaker. More applause rang through the room and, once it had diminished, he observed someone standing at microphone number one.

"Mr. Moderator, what about the lost? I speak against the change in policy out of a concern for lost people who have a genetic predisposition to strong drink. We have seen many of such folks come to Christ and get set free from the desire to drink. Shall we moderately indulge in that from which they abstain? Besides, moderation is an elusive standard . . ."

And so it continued.

Debate followed for another half hour. Finally, when it seemed nearly too much, a young man approached microphone number four. Reverend Micks recognized him and motioned him to speak.

"Mr. Moderator," he began. "I want to thank the Committee on Theological Issues for their hard work in coming up with a revision to our policy on abstinence from alcohol among licensed workers. I imagine that the simple statement they have presented took many hours to craft. They have my and I assume the entire constituency's appreciation at attempting a feat fraught with challenges." The young man paused to look around the room as though to acknowledge those who had crafted the statement.

"Let me get straight to my point. I have a confession to make. I and a cohort of like-minded friends lobbied for this change since our last General Assembly. We worked tirelessly to pave the way for its passage at this meeting. We believed that the current policy limited the potential pool of future ministers in our denomination. We saw this as a stumbling block. Our zeal for changing the policy was pragmatic, the staffing of our churches and the survival of our movement. We also justified our efforts by believing that the old policy was archaic. We believed it reflected an outdated secondary issue, one that did not affect our core doctrines."

"After listening to those who have spoken for and against this issue, my cohort and I have consulted with each other and confirmed that this is indeed a secondary issue. And, as such, we now see that leaving the existing policy in place is as viable as changing it. In pursuing a change in policy we do not wish to jeopardize the spiritual wellbeing of some within our body who would stumble over this change. Neither would we want to divide our body to gain a hollow victory. We do not have answers as to how we can better recruit younger ministers to fill our pulpits. However, we are willing to trust the Lord with you that He will provide the personnel we need without changing our policy. We have no desire to offend good brothers and sisters who may struggle with alcohol or whose families suffered because of it."

"We would also confess that we have belittled some of our forefathers for coming up with this policy in the first place. Sometimes in seeking to do what one believes to be the right thing, he or she may overlook the love such changes require. We feel we may have crossed the line in pursuing our will in this matter. We beg the assembly's forgiveness for any grief or division we have caused. We release our proposal that the policy be changed."

As the speaker stepped back from the microphone the entire auditorium sat in pin-drop silence. And then, like a thunder clap on a blue sky day, the room erupted in applause!

Reverend Micks seemed stunned. He struggled to gain the attention of the assembly. *Knock! Knock! Knock! Knock!* He frantically pounded his gavel on the podium. As things began to settle down, someone yelled, "Question!" To which Reverend Micks replied, "The question has been called for."

He went on, "Brothers and sisters, before we take up the vote on the proposed policy change, I want to ask another personal privilege and invite our denominational president to pray over what is about to transpire."

Unlike his name, Dr. Stephen Steadman appeared anything but steady. He rose from his seat and limped his way to the podium, cane in hand. His voice raspy, not from age but from trial and hardship, he asked the entire assembly to join him in prayer. After a pause, he began:

"Heavenly Father, You raised up this movement many years ago. Yet today feels like a hinge moment in our experience. It seems so, not because the issue we will vote on changes the course of our future. It does not. This moment's significance lay in the way we have addressed the issue together. We have managed to discuss a difficult topic, one laced with the threat of division, without harshness or judgmentalism. And now, by Your grace, we anticipate a result that will transform a stumbling stone into a stepping stone toward greater unity. We thank You for that! We thank You for the leadership of our moderator, Reverend Micks who guided us prayerfully through the process."

"Now, oh Lord, something has come out in these discussions for which I must take responsibility. It has come out, and I believe truthfully so, that we have at times in our history given into the spirit of legalism. Today, I stand in the place of all those who have held this office before me, some of whom may have led imperfectly. I am just as capable of doing the same. However, in this moment I want to ask Your forgiveness for us as leaders allowing the spirit of legalism to mar our relationships with each other, with the world and with *You*. Forgive us for our pharisaical attitudes which have been a part of our movement from its founding. Oh Lord, heal us from any wounds we have suffered as a body that flow from man-made rules. Create in us a clean heart and renew a right spirit within us. We commit ourselves and the outcome of this vote to You. In Jesus' precious name. Amen."

Sniffles, tears and hugs broke out across the auditorium as the tellers passed out the ballots.

## Back at Fairway

Pastor Griff strolled pensively into the boardroom for staff meeting. Like before, he was the first to arrive and again began to pace. This time he had one arm across his chest and the other propped above it, his hand stroking his beard. He had been so struck by the way the discussion about the policy on abstinence had gone at General Assembly that he pondered the implications for his "Green Church Service" idea. Maybe he and his staff could get on the same page after all.

Within a few moments the same cast of clergy sat in their own places around the conference table. Griff began, "So what did you guys think about that discussion at General Assembly about changing the abstinence policy?"

Rob jumped right in. "Griff" he began, "We all knew that discussion was on the agenda. Most of us were dreading it. I still cannot get over how two such opposing agendas could come together in tangible unity."

Seth thought about poking Rob, since the discussion was about beverages, but he had been so impacted by the Tuesday afternoon session at General Assembly that he let the opportunity pass. Instead he echoed Rob's sentiment, "I have never seen such a divisive issue result in unified action. I still shake my head when I think about it. We've all seen these lobbies for one issue or another at General Assembly before. They never turn out pretty. And after President Steadman's prayer the spirit of the meetings completely changed. The services seemed more anointed, the singing more inspired. It seemed as if God was honoring the way things went down."

Tom, who usually did everything by the book, was equally affected. "Did you notice they neglected to perfectly follow *Robert's Rules of Order?* They did not do things the 'right way' and God still blessed it. I was getting irritated with all the 'special privileges' the moderator requested, but how could I argue with the result?"

Zack, chimed in. "Think of that. *Robert's Rules of Order* violated, and God still showed up. I don't mean to be funny, but it is. How do we deconstruct what happened?"

Griff gave it a try. "Did you notice that Reverend Micks was upfront about how sensitive the issue was? Then he engaged us all in prayer ahead of the discussion. Somehow it had a humbling effect on everyone."

Seth added, "Yes, and people felt the freedom to speak. Perhaps more importantly they had the opportunity to be *heard*. Some addressed the pastoral aspects of the change and others focused on the doctrinal or teaching aspects. One guy shared his testimony of how alcohol impacted his family. He exuded the gift of mercy."

Rob spoke. "I thought the first speaker was particularly discerning. How would God view the change if the original pledge to abstain from alcohol had been made to *Him*? I had never considered it from that angle."

Griff added, "Two things impressed me. One was how the whole room responded when the cohort that pushed for the change released their demand. Somehow that cohort recognized what the Spirit was saying through the rest of the speakers. They chose to align with the Spirit, sacrificing their agenda. The other thing that I can't get out of my mind was Dr. Steadman's prayer right before the vote. The speaker who mentioned our history of legalism spoke like a prophet to the heart of our denomination. Then, Steadman confessed the sins of legalism by past leaders as if they were his own. I think that's when the spirit of the meetings changed."

It was then that Rob tied all this to Griff's new ministry idea for Fairway Church. "I can't help contrasting the dissonance we experienced in our last staff meeting about the Jumbotron ministry with the resonance we witnessed Tuesday at General Assembly. I think we need to revisit the golf cart church service idea and use some of the principles we witnessed at General Assembly."

"Like what?" Tom asked.

Rob replied, "Like humbling ourselves in prayer the way we did before we discussed the whole abstinence topic. There was a yielding of agendas in those prayers that allowed people to share without the threat of judgment. I also think we should expect people to have different perspectives on the issue, like they did. But instead of settling for discordant viewpoints, or a shallow outcome guided by Robert's Rules of Order, we should realize that the Holy Spirit may be speaking through all of us. We just need to sense how all our perspectives tie into His."

Griff couldn't help his next comment. "I'll have whatever Rob is drinking." The whole group laughed together. Then Griff added, "Well, maybe we have our first taste of that resonance Rob mentioned."

Tom cleared his throat and everyone stiffened a little. "Guys, I want to ask your forgiveness for my heavy-handed approach to Griff's Jumbotron idea. Like the one guy who shared about his family that was impacted by alcohol, mine was too. As a result, I've been afflicted with a need to control my environment ever since. Money was always a source of conflict in my home and I'm afraid I have not always handled the topic in a Spirit-guided fashion."

Griff felt something let loose in his spirit. Was it compassion? Was it grief? Maybe it was that if Tom could confess his harshness, perhaps he was not as much like Griff's abusive dad as he thought.

Griff replied, "Tom, you don't know how much that means to me. Not because it gets me closer to a new ministry idea, but because I have been reacting to you out of my own painful relationship with *my* father. I need to ask you to forgive me, brother."

The room grew quiet and the moment became sacred. The Holy Spirit was in the room, filling the space and the conversation. Seth began to pray. "Oh Lord, You have answered our prayer for wisdom from last week. It was not in a way any of us expected. But here we sit, some of us in tears. Lord, You are unifying us, not around an agenda, but around Your Spirit working in and through each of us. Forgive us for not valuing the spiritual gifts You have placed in each of us. Heal us from any past wounds that limit our ability to love each other or to be fully useful to you. Lord, whether we are sitting outside worshipping you in front of a Jumbotron or not, we want You to be in the center of our efforts. Help us to hear what You are saying to us as leaders and as a church."

The room was quiet for a long time. Tom finally broke the sacred silence. "You know Griff, as we were praying the Lord seemed to tell me to turn the church's finances over to Him. Maybe there's a Jumbotron in our future after all."

# Chapter 9 Discsussion Questions:

1. What would you say were Griff's, Tom's, Zack's, Seth's and Rob's spiritual gifts?

2. How did those gifts work together or against each other prior to General Assembly?

3. What spiritual gifts were evident in the discussion at the General Assembly?

4. What signs of resonance do you witness in the account of the General Assembly?

5. Why do you think the spirit of the General Assembly changed?

6. When did dissonance change to resonance during the second staff meeting at Fairway Church?

7. What role did the Holy Spirit play in the second staff meeting at Fairway?

8. What lessons you can take from this story?

We welcome your honest feedback. Would you take a moment to write a brief review of *The Dance of the Gifts* on its Amazon page?

Thank you!

# Acknowledgements

No author is an island. While our names may be on the cover, this book's publications was aided by two special people. Thank you, Debbie Smith, for once again applying your eagle eye and administrative gifts to another one of our manuscripts. You bless us with your gifts of encouragement and service! Mitch Schultz, your descriptive powers helped bring the last chapter to life. Your ministry to hurting pastors, which I am happy to mention here, reflects your gift of encouragement (fruitfulvineministry.com).

# Bibliography

Barnard, Mark. *The Path of Revival: Restoring our Nation One Church at a Time.* Chicago: ChurchSmart, 2009.

Barnard, Mark and Kenneth Quick. *The Eighth Letter: Jesus Still Speaks – What is He saying to Your Church?* Chicago: ChurchSmart, 2014.

Dallimore, Arnold. *George Whitefield: The Life and Times of the Great Evangelist of the 18th Century Revival.* London: Banner of Truth, 2001.

Edwards, Jonathan. *A Narrative of Surprising Conversions.* London: Banner of Truth, 1965.

Friedman, Edwin H. *A Failure of Nerve.* New York: Church Publishing, 2017.

Fee, Gordon D. *Listening to the Spirit in the Text.* Grand Rapids: Eerdmans, 2000.

Guinness, Os. *The Call* Nashville: Thomas Nelson, 1998.

Hughes, R. Kent. *Acts: The Church Afire.* Wheaton: Crossways, 1996.

Lloyd-Jones, Martyn. *Joy Unspeakable.* Wheaton: Harold Shaw, 1984.

Macleod, Donald. *The Person of Christ.* Downers Grove, IL: IVP, 1998.

Quick, Kenneth. *Body Aches: Experiencing and Responding to God's Discipline of Your Church.* Chicago: ChurchSmart, 2009.

Quick, Kenneth. *Healing the Heart of Your Church (second edition). Createspace,* 2018.

Quick, Kenneth. *Living for the Kingdom: Eternal Significance as Motivation for the Christian Life,* available digitally on Logos at https://www.logos.com/product/25966/living-for-the-kingdom-eternal-significance-as-motivation-for-the-christian-life

Torrey, R.A. *The Person and Word of the Holy Spirit.* New York: Revell.

Made in USA - Kendallville, IN
1085062_9781654567507
04.22.2020.0708